Big Impact

Big Brothers Making a Difference

Richard S. Greif

Published by
New Hat Publishing
P.O. Box 2464
Boston, MA 02208
(617)628-2872

www.ppsa.com/newhat/

Printed in the United States of America

Library of Congress Catalog Number: 97-67515
ISBN: 0-9658310-02

Dedication

This book is dedicated to:

All Big Brothers Big Sisters agencies and their staffs—Thank you for the work you do every day and the tireless effort you put into recruiting, fundraising, supporting matches, and most importantly, promoting the interests of children. I hope this book takes us one giant step further to serving all the boys who need a Big Brother.

All Big Brothers, past, present, and future—Thank you for taking the time to share the gifts of caring, concern, and friendship, and for opening your hearts to all that Little Brothers have to offer. Your efforts will always make a difference.

All current and former Little Brothers—Thank you for giving your Big Brothers a chance to share their lives with you. Your smiles, humor, and hope for the future make every moment worthwhile for your Big Brothers.

All mothers and guardians of Little Brothers—Thank you for courageously opening your hearts and trusting Big Brothers Big Sisters to bring additional support and friendship into your sons' lives.

And last, but far from least, this book is dedicated to *the thousands of boys waiting for a Big Brother.* I hope your days will soon be filled with laughter and joy from time spent with a Big Brother.

Contents

Preface

"100 years from now. . . it will not matter what your bank account was, the sort of house you lived in, or the kind of car you drive, but the world may be different because you were important in the life of a child."

Anonymous

As a boy, my father and my grandfather were my two primary male influences. My father spent most of his time working, and his success and work ethic provided a standard that I measure myself against to this day. My grandfather, who lived near us, spent a lot of time with me—talking, playing sports, and taking great pride in my accomplishments. He would do just about anything to help me, no questions asked. My grandfather never judged or criticized me; he loved me for who I was. Although my father and grandfather are no longer alive, I cannot imagine where I would be or how I would have turned out if I had not had them in my life. Their combined influence helped me raise the bar of expectations on myself and who I could become.

All over the United States, millions of boys lack the kind of loving support and guidance I received from caring men. Research tells us over and over that boys living in single-parent families are much more likely than other children to commit crimes, join gangs, abuse drugs, and fall behind in or drop out of school. Such boys often exhibit behavior and learning problems and produce children out of wedlock.

In previous generations adults watched out for each other's children, and families lived closer together. Today such extended support networks are rare. A recent advertising survey found that 75 percent of Americans do not know the name of their next door neighbor. As a nation, we have become strong on individual rights and weak on community obligation. Adults have less and less time to devote to children in school, at home, and in our communities.

People no longer feel a sense of commitment and obligation to others. As a friend of mine reminded me recently, "Not only do we not have parents watching out for children, we no longer have anyone in the community reinforcing the types of values and behaviors we say we want." As a result, children have few people to turn to in times of crisis or tension, fewer homes to play in, and fewer adults to meet, mingle with, and be mentored by.

One Man; One Boy

For the past six years, I have had the privilege of being involved with a program that makes relationships possible, Big Brothers Big Sisters of America. As a Big Brother, I have experienced firsthand the need that many boys have for adult male friendship and support. By befriending one boy for just a few hours a week, men not only make a difference in boys' lives, but in their families, in the community, and in their own lives. A Big Brother alone will not entirely change a boy's life, but research now proves that having a Big Brother clearly makes a positive difference and is a significant step in the right direction. (See Appendix II, page 147 for a report of the research conducted by Public Private Ventures (PPV), which proves the effectiveness of Big Brothers Big Sisters programs.)

The motivation to write this book came from a former Little Brother I met about two summers ago. On a sunny Saturday afternoon, I was playing touch football with my Little Brother Tony and some of his friends. During a break in the game, one of the boys' fathers came over to me and asked if I was Tony's Big Brother. Not thinking anything of it, I replied, "Yes I am, why do you ask?"

The man told me that he had been a Little Brother some 25 years ago and that the Big Brothers program had a huge impact on his life. When he was ten years old, he was living with his mother. His older brother was in jail, and his sister was in drug and alcohol rehabilitation. His father was abusive and had left the family when the man was young. As a result, this boy did poorly in school and frequently got into trouble. Essentially, he was heading down the same path as his siblings. His mother decided that he might benefit from male influence, so she applied to have him matched with a Big Brother.

The man went on to tell me how his Big Brother literally opened new doors for him. Having a Big Brother came at a very critical time in his life, because he figured he was just going to end up the same way his family had. Although he and his Big Brother were only matched for three years, he learned that there were many options and choices in the world. He also learned that there was much more to the world than what existed on his street corner and in his neighborhood. His Big Brother taught him that he could be anything he wanted to be, and that the only person who could stop him was himself. That man now works for a large corporation in Boston, lives in a good community, and has a wife and three children.

As we finished our conversation, the man told me he regretted that he did not know where his Big Brother was now. He told me that he probably did not appreciate what his Big Brother did for him at the time. He said simply, "But when I heard you were a Big Brother, I wanted to come over to tell you how much I appreciate what you're doing for your Little Brother, because I know one day he will appreciate what you have done for him."

A Desperate Need for Caring Men

The Big Brothers Big Sisters organization serves more than 100,000 boys and girls throughout America. Many men enjoy the benefits of being Big Brothers. But there is a desperate need for many, many more good men to step forward and brother the boys who wait.

Nearly two-thirds of all waiting lists at Big Brothers Big Sisters agencies across the country are boys waiting for Big Brothers. Many wait one to three years, while some boys grow too old for the program and never get a Big Brother. My Little Brother Tony has two brothers, Charles and Andrew, who have been waiting years for a Big Brother. They have all but given up hope. For them and the other thousands of boys waiting for a Big Brother, every day is a missed opportunity.

Many boys in single-parent families spend much of their lives without fathers. While I cannot influence fathers to become reengaged with their sons, what I can advocate is the reengagement of adult males in the lives of boys—not as substitute fathers or disciplinarians, but as the caring, supportive adult males boys so desperately need and crave. This is in no way meant to diminish the importance of single mothers; it is merely an acknowledgment that adult men can and do play a critical role in helping boys decide which life path they will follow.

I have written this book for the sole purpose of introducing men to the phenomenon of Big Brotherhood. This is a story that invites men to make a difference in the lives of children—and in their own lives. I am offering much more than "15 minutes of fame." Rather, my invitation—my challenge—guarantees hours, days, weeks, months, and years of importance in the heart of a child.

Please read this book with an open mind and an open heart. Thoughtfully consider the men and boys you meet here. And then generously, courageously, and selfishly, look into your typical week and decide if you have three or four hours available to change someone's life. You cannot even imagine the rewards that await you.

One more request. When you have finished the book, and you have made your decision—whatever it is—do one more thing. Pass it on. Give the book to another good man, so that he might have the opportunity to learn about the magic of the Big Brother experience.

Each One Teach One

This book is a call for human action and reaction. It is simply an invitation to learn more about how good caring men can make a difference in the lives of our nation's boys. It is time for all of us to answer the call of the Presidents' Summit on America's Future, held April 27–29, 1997, where President and Mrs. Clinton, former First Lady Nancy Reagan, former President and Mrs. Ford, former President and Mrs. Carter, retired General Colin Powell, and 2,500 citizen leaders kicked off an unprecedented effort to secure our children's future through grassroots citizen action against the many problems facing us as a society. The Summit's stated goals were "to provide young people with five fundamental resources—an ongoing relationship with a caring adult mentor; safe places and structured activities during non-school hours; adequate medical care and healthy behavior; a marketable skill through education; and an opportunity to give back through community service." Or as Colin Powell stated, the Summit is a call for each one to teach one. "We will reach down, we will reach back, we will reach across to help our brothers and sisters in need," said General Powell. I hope this book spurs you to action to help the Presidents' Summit reach its goals, and I want it to further the discussion of the importance of having adult men actively involved in the development of our boys.

The Big Impact Story

Initially this book provides some background on the origin of Big Brothers Big Sisters of America. You will be introduced to the types of men, boys, and families that get involved with Big Brothers Big Sisters. You will learn what a Big/Little Brother "match" is like, how it is formed, and the types of activities that Bigs and Littles do. You'll see what it takes to be a Big Brother, and learn some tips on how to have a successful relationship with a Little Brother. Most importantly, you'll get a glimpse of how the program affects Little Brothers, Big Brothers, their families, and society. Finally, you'll read about other ways to assist local Big Brothers Big Sisters agencies. Throughout the book, I will share with you some of the wonderful memories and stories I have collected over the past year and a half.

Most of the insight in the book comes directly from the experts, the people who are involved with Big Brothers Big Sisters programs from around the country. I interviewed and spent time with more than 200 current and former Big Brothers, Little Brothers, Mothers, and Big Brothers Big Sisters agency staff. I worked directly with more than 150 Big Brothers Big Sisters agencies in 40 states. The themes and messages throughout the book are theirs. I am not a psychologist, social research scientist, or caseworker. I am simply a Big Brother who believes that this is one of the finest youth programs around that has, for more than 90 years, successfully contributed to the positive development of boys and girls. The Big Brothers Big Sisters approach is simple: provide supportive adult attention for kids, and more often than not, positive behaviors result.

I wish I had the space to introduce you to more of the many people whose caring and thoughtfulness represent everything that could be good in the world if we just opened our hearts a little bit. Knowing these people has made writing this book one of the greatest gifts I will ever receive.

Becoming a Big Brother

Robert Kennedy once said, "Few will have the greatness to bend history itself, but each of us can work to change a small portion of events, and in the total of all those acts will be written the history of this generation." As individuals, we cannot help everyone. But that does not mean we cannot help one person. We have a say in the creation of our history.

If you, like me, worry about our nation's boys and have wondered how you can make a difference, I invite you to share the experiences of those who have done just that. This book is about how men, by just being themselves and nothing more, can make a significant difference in a boy's life—a Big Impact.

When I became a Big Brother in 1991, my hope was to make a dif-ference in a boy's life. What I did not realize is the difference it would make in my life. Being a Big Brother to Tony is about much more than the activities we do. I have had the pleasure of watching an energetic 9-year-old boy grow into a caring, hopeful 15-year-old man. My role since day one has been to listen, be supportive, but most of all, to just be there. Tony still has many hills to climb, but he knows he is never alone. In return for a little bit of my time, I have received a plethora of great memories and a special friendship that money could never buy. While I cannot predict what will happen to either of us, I know for sure that we are both better off because of our time together.

And this is how it all began. . . .

Big Impact: Rich and Tony

The First Meeting—July 1, 1991

Today I will meet my Little Brother, Tony, for the first time. No, this is not a long lost relative of mine. Rather, it will be my first meeting with my Little Brother through the Big Brother Association of Greater Boston. As I leave work on this sunny July day to drive down to meet him, his family, and our caseworker, all sorts of thoughts race through my head. What will he be like? Will he like me? What will his family be like? What should we do? How should I act? While I have had these thoughts for awhile, as I contemplate them now, I realize that I am anxious and excited that the day has finally come.

I have wanted to be a Big Brother for some time. The fact that I never had a brother certainly was a major factor in my deci-sion to apply. Both my desire to give something back to the community and my ability to relate to children inspired me. All in all, I was extremely fortunate growing up, and yet I see many smart, talented children who do not get the support and encour-agement they need and deserve.

There is something energizing and refreshing about being around children. They are more honest, direct, and straightfor-ward than most adults. They live life for the moment, have fun, and enjoy it, as opposed to many adults who often have forgotten what it means to simply play and have fun.

And so, despite the fact that I am in a very time-consuming, demanding job, I do not see sharing a few hours a week with someone as a big commitment. In fact, given all the other challenges and pressures I face in life, this is a great opportunity for me to grow as an individual, and also to kick back and enjoy the free time.

As I pull up near Tony's house and meet the caseworker, I grow even more anxious. She reassures me that everything will go fine, and tells me again that we will spend a little bit of time together as a group (with her and Tony's grandmother), and after that my Little Brother and I should go off and spend some time on our own.

When I walk in, Tony's grandmother is very pleasant and cordial to me, and she tries to encourage my new Little Brother to say something. He is a small, very shy, 9-year-old, with little to say for now. While this is overwhelming for me, I realize he probably has little idea of what is going on himself. All he knows is I am some guy who has come to spend time with him. But what does that mean to him?

We all make small talk for awhile, and Tony is giving typical one-word answers to all the questions— "Yes." "No." "Good." With the initial introductions over, it is finally time for the two of us to be alone. We go out to the backyard and talk. I try to uncover what his interests are, and they seem typical for his age—most sports, video games, and movies.

I felt like I was running out of questions to ask when Tony asked me if I wanted to play kickball. Recalling my elementary school years, I quickly take on his challenge. I soon learn that Tony is the best on his block. We played for what seemed like hours. You could tell by the energy in his face that he was not taking this lightly, that he was going to establish just who Tony Merrill was. In the end, despite my best efforts, I think I lost something like 14–13. From time to time, I noticed Tony's grandmother watching through the window, eyeing the two of us curiously. Whoever would have thought that I would be playing kickball again in my 20s?

Before I realized it, a couple of hours had gone by, and it was getting late. Tony and I discussed what we might do on our next meeting, and we set a date and time. I gave him my phone number and told him to call me if he felt like it or if he ever needed to, otherwise I'd just see him next week. I figured that I would probably give him a call before our next meeting.

I drove home with a pretty good feeling that our first encounter had gone well. Tony seemed like an energetic kid and, although he has had a challenging childhood, I hoped that would make little difference to our friendship.

When I got home and checked my answering machine, there was one long message. To my surprise, it was Tony. He must have talked for about ten minutes, going on and on about various things. He rattled off all sorts of miscellaneous facts about things he knew or liked or did not like. I listened to the message and tried to imagine him on the phone at his house talking to me. More than anything, that message made me realize that all Tony really wants is someone to listen to him, spend time with him, show interest in him, and care about how he feels.

And even now, in our sixth year of friendship, I realize that these simple practices are still, and always will be, the most important things I can do for Tony.

Richard S. Greif
Boston, Massachusetts
May 1997

Acknowledgments

When I first developed the concept for this book, I was unsure of the reaction I would receive. While I have been a volunteer Big Brother for six years, that pales in comparison to the decades of work accomplished by the devoted professionals at Big Brothers Big Sisters agencies. What I discovered is that Big Brothers Big Sisters is a tremendous support network across the country.

Several people were very encouraging when I first discussed the idea for this book. Thank you to John Pearson, executive director of the Big Brothers Association of Greater Boston, and Viola Bostic and Tom McKenna and all the staff from Big Brothers Big Sisters of America for being receptive to my thoughts. A tremendous thank you to all the Big Brothers Big Sisters agencies and their staffs, board members, and volunteers for their involvement in this project. As they showered me with letters, phone calls, faxes, and e-mails, they demonstrated both their commitment to advancing the mission of Big Brothers Big Sisters and an important faith and trust that I would do my best to further that mission. A special thank you to all who took the time to be interviewed for this book. The opportunity to listen to them open their hearts and share their experiences was a gift I will always treasure.

Thank you to all the good friends who sustained me throughout this project. Their constant support provided much needed encouragement at critical junctures. A special thank you to all of my friends at Insight Boston for supporting me and giving me the tools to trust and believe in myself. Thank you also to the members of the band, Shakedaddy, for encouraging me to develop my musical ability as another outlet of expression. A big thank you goes to all of my family for believing in me and supporting me, especially my mother, grandmother, and great uncles. Thank you also to Larry Litwak of Greif, Litwak, and Bartlett, P.C., for his advice, encouragement, and support, and to Jill Charles and the folks at the Dorset Writer's Colony in Vermont for hosting me this past fall.

Immeasurable thanks to my Little Brother Tony Merrill. Throughout our six years of friendship, Tony has always been there for me. When the idea of this book progressed, he immediately expressed his support and has been a constant inspiration to me. Without Tony this book would not have been possible.

Thank you also to Janice, Graham, Pat, Theresa, Rob, Barb, Gloria, and all of the staff at Professional Resources & Communications for their work in the editing and design of this book. Their professionalism, efficiency, and attention to detail have added a new level of quality to this book. Thank you to my good friend Richard Schultz for the outstanding cover photography.

In every project, there is always at least one person who provides constant support, guidance, and faith; someone who shares the successes, but is also there when the chips are down; someone who picks you up, throws you back in the ring, and believes in you when you need it most. For me that person is a wonderful woman named Katherine Cruise. From moment one, she steadfastly demonstrated her belief in me, and often had more confidence in me than I had. Katherine supported me in taking a chance to leave an unfulfilling career and pursue a dream. This book would not be what it is without her, and I will never be able to thank her enough.

It is also important for me to acknowledge my own efforts in making this book a reality. Writing this book was a tremendous stretch out of my comfort zone. I took a chance by leaving a stable career to pursue a goal—not only to advance the mission of Big Brothers, but to find a place in the world where I could match my skills and talents with something that I truly believed in. Creating this book was the ideal win/win/win scenario for me and has helped me achieve goals that I once only dreamed of accomplishing. I hope that my work has a Big Impact on the lives of countless boys and men for years to come. And I hope that this book, the beginning of my dream come true, will encourage others to follow their hearts.

≥◎≤   ≥◎≤   ≥◎≤

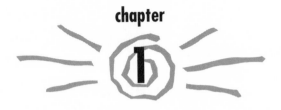

chapter 1

Beginnings

"It's important that today's kids find a role model. They need to

see the positive. They grasp on to their environment, and they

do what their environment tells them. If you have a positive

role model, you can look at them and see there's more than

drugs and negative things. There's a straight road, a positive

road. That's why we support Big Brothers Big Sisters of

America."

Wanya Morris, member of Boyz II Men
Big Brothers Big Sisters of America Annual Report 1995

≥⊙≤   ≥⊙≤   ≥⊙≤

Big Impact:
Kenny Gordon and Phillip Henry

Chattanooga Big Brothers Big Sisters, Tennessee

Imagine living in a world of poverty, resentment, and violence with little exposure to anything better and no reason for hope. Then one day you come upon this magical machine, and you put your quarter in and all of a sudden you're in the world of plenty, without any worries or misfortunes.[1]

Phillip Henry's "magical machine" turned out to be a man named Kenny Gordon, who became his Big Brother back in 1983. Phillip was just seven years old at the time he was matched with Kenny. Phillip lived with his mother and never knew his father. He lived in surroundings that were filled with crime, violence, and poverty. Kenny, who co-owns a jewelry store with his brother, became a Big Brother in part because of the close relationship he had with his own father who died when Kenny was 27.

Phillip and Kenny both remember their first time together. They went out for ice cream and talked about Phillip's second grade class and the fact that he particularly liked math. Kenny remembers Phillip as a shy child. Since Phillip had never really had any consistent male figures in his life, he thought that Kenny must have been paid to be his friend. He had no idea at the time what the word "volunteer" meant. But that thought would change in time.

"Kenny was the exception to the rule. He stuck with me through thick and thin. I eventually began to trust him, but it took a long time. He surprised me with his great endurance. I remember what a milestone it was to reach our first year together. I was surprised. Kenny had the patience and understanding to look past the welfare and food stamps and see a little boy 'rich' with ambition and drive to do something in the world."[2]

Kenny and Phillip have shared many pleasant journeys together, and Kenny introduced as many new cultural experiences to Phillip as possible. While they occasionally went on special trips to places like Disney World and New York, they often spent time enjoying simple pastimes like fishing. "*Kenny opened the door to opportunity after opportunity. He also began to put some culture in a very uncultured person,*" *recalls Phillip.*

"*I have opened some doors for Phillip but he has taken advantage of every opportunity,*" *says Kenny.* "*I've helped guide Phillip, but he's always had the right attitude—the desire to do and be his best.*"

For Phillip, every meeting with Kenny was an opportunity. "*I realized every time was a chance to get out of the house and do something different and learn something new,*" *says Phillip.*

Kenny was instrumental in helping Phillip experience some unique programs, like a trip to Mark Twain's home in Hannibal, Missouri. Kenny spoke with the Nature Center in Chattanooga, which was running the trip, and they helped arrange a scholarship for Phillip and other children. Another summer Phillip attended Space Camp on scholarship, with Kenny arranging for many people's support, including their Congresswoman. Phillip was also part of a select group chosen to work in the Youth Conservation Corp. of Yellowstone National Park. There he built bridges and hiked over 100 miles of trails. From this experience, he learned that living up to his own expectations and following what was in his heart were the right ways to live.

Kenny was instrumental in helping Phillip get into Baylor, an elite prep school in Tennessee. Because of Phillip's hard work and positive attitude, he was able to get a complete scholarship for all four years. Phillip would go on to graduate with honors. He is currently a junior at the University of Georgia, and this summer he will travel to Ecuador to study Spanish.

"*I have gone through a great deal of self-realization and have concluded that I have gained from my experiences, and I am committed to turning my life around from an unfortunate background to a promising future. My mother's actions and experiences have made me strong and ready to endure anything. Kenny's lifestyle has also helped me conclude that whatever I want is out there. I just have to reach for it. These two lifestyles put together have given me the greatest drive and ambition a person could have, while at the same time always reminding me never to take anything for granted.*"[3]

Compared to his peers growing up, Phillip can say he's doing pretty well for himself. "*Most of the kids from the old neighbor-*

hood are just working or hanging out. I only know one other per-son I grew up with who's going to college," says Phillip.

Over their 14 years of friendship, Kenny has watched Phillip evolve from a child lacking self-confidence to a well-adjusted college student with a bright future.

"Phillip's shyness and low self-esteem slowly dissipated through the constant encouragement, patience, and guidance that only a loving friendship can provide. Each bit of encour-agement and every victory brought out the right attitude, the polite mannerisms, and the unbridled ambition that would one day drive Phillip to his own achievements. But perhaps my great-est gift to Phillip was instilling the belief that a better future was possible for him if only he would go for it. You don't know what you can do until you try, but you've got to keep trying. And so, through the years, we bonded, building a relationship of trust and respect for one another, and doors of opportunity opened for us. The beauty of volunteering for a good cause is the help peo-ple are so willing to give to those who are willing to help themselves. The American Dream is to reach out to others with a helping hand and to provide the guidance and leadership that enable their dreams to come true."[4]

Being a Big Brother has had just as big an impact on Kenny. "I have always enjoyed getting together with Phillip. It has given my life a bigger sense of purpose and meaning." And although Kenny now has a new Little Brother, Ryan, his third Little Brother with Chattanooga Big Brothers Big Sisters in Tennessee, he believes that he and Phillip will be friends forever. "Phillip's like my own son, a part of my family. We'll always be close."

Kenny Gordon and Phillip Henry, two friends together make a Big Impact.

$$\geqslant \widehat{6} \leqslant \quad \geqslant \widehat{6} \leqslant \quad \geqslant \widehat{6} \leqslant$$

A New Approach

Some boys grow up with a combination of opportunities and resources to help guide and support them, such as family, peers, reli-gious and youth organizations, social agencies, and schools. But many boys do not have such support. These boys face tremendous chal-lenges caused by deteriorating family structures, unpleasant living conditions, and a challenging socioeconomic status. In the past a boy could expect to be mentored by his teachers, parents, and extended family. Today boys without these resources approach life with what is available to them, unless there is someone willing to help them become aware of what the world holds.

Mentoring programs have emerged as a means of filling this support gap. Emphasis has been placed on finding capable adults who are willing and able to share time and friendship in the hope of improving the future of children. Since nearly the beginning of the century, boys and girls have been mentored through Big Brothers Big Sisters programs all across America.

The Origin of Big Brothers[5]

Big Brothers Big Sisters of America, the modern federation of more than 500 affiliated Big Brothers Big Sisters agencies, officially traces its roots to the work of Ernest K. Coulter who helped organize the first Children's Court in New York City. As clerk of that court, Ernest was appalled by the number of children passing through the courts, only to return again and again. He saw little if any concern being shown to the children's individual circumstances. Ernest reviewed the records of the New York City Children's Court and noticed that many of the boys who had come into contact with the court came from fatherless homes. Ernest decided that the influence of a man in the lives of each of these youngsters would help curb their behavior.

On December 3, 1904, Ernest spoke about his beliefs to a men's club of the Central Presbyterian Church of New York, which included many of the area's business, professional, and community leaders. He discussed one particular boy who had been brought into the court who was destined for 18 months in a reformatory.

"There is only one possible way to save that youngster," Ernest said, "and that is to have some earnest, true man volunteer to be his Big Brother, to look after him, help him do right, make the little chap feel that there is one human being in the great city who takes a personal interest in him, who cares whether he lives or dies. I call for a volunteer."

From that meeting 40 men resolved to initiate a relationship with a boy from the court caseload, including the boy Ernest had described. Activity continued to spread throughout New York City, and in 1909 some of these same men joined Ernest in formally incorporating the first

Big Brothers' agency in the nation, Big Brothers of New York City, Inc.

The guidelines formed at that time included: "Be interested in the boy's interests. Invite him to your office and to your home, take him to the ball game, a concert, or a good clean show. Get him interested in one of the boys' gymnasiums, and if you find your Little Brother has a bent in any particular direction, give him a chance to exercise it. Above all things, do not patronize. Just be a brother and a companion to your boy. Give the boy his individual chance to be honest and to grow up to be a useful citizen."

Ernest also reminded the first Big Brothers that their primary function was to provide friendship. "A large percentage of boys . . . don't have a decent friend in the world to help them. What the boys want are friends, not charity," said Ernest in a 1909 *Good Housekeeping* article.[6]

Saving Boys in Cincinnati

It was just outside of his office, on the Fourth of July, 1903, that Irvin F. Westheimer, a 23-year-old Cincinnati businessman, unwittingly launched another Big Brothers movement. "I began the holiday by researching the Declaration of Independence. A phrase stuck in my mind: 'All men are created equal.' I couldn't stop thinking about it. Those were more sentimental times," said Irvin.

At the time Irvin was operating the Cincinnati branch of his father's business, and he went down to the office as usual, even though it was Independence Day. After working awhile at his big old roll-top desk, Irvin happened to look out the window. He saw a young, curly-haired boy scavenging in garbage cans. The boy was fishing for morsels of food and sharing them with his dog. Irvin rushed downstairs to see what he could do, and he promptly introduced himself.

"My name is Irv."

"I'm Tom."

"What's your dog's name?"

"Gyp."

Tom and Irv talked awhile, and Irv learned that Tom was one of five children, "with a father gone or dead and a mother working something akin to desperation."

Irvin took the boy to a restaurant and fed him, then went home to ponder that quotation, "All men are created equal." "Indeed! Things must have been different in Thomas Jefferson's day!" thought Irv.

The following week Irv went to Tom's home and met his family. With his mother's permission, Irv took Tom to see the Reds play baseball and began taking him on various outings. Irv was enjoying his time with Tom, and he could tell it was doing a lot for the boy as well.

When Irv realized that other fatherless boys could be helped in a similar way, he began talking about the idea. "I soon had all my friends—Cincinnati businessmen—'adopting' boys too," said Irv. Wherever he traveled on business, Irv spent his evenings acquainting other men with the idea and setting up groups in those towns to help young fatherless boys. "The boys started calling us their Big Brothers. So, when the group was formally organized, that was the name we adopted," said Irv.

This experience led to the organization of a Big Brothers agency in Cincinnati in 1910. Irvin Westheimer disclosed that Tom had been in reform school twice before he had found him but that now, nearly eight years later, he was not only supporting his family, he was also devoting both his time and money to charity.

Irv described Big Brothers as "big-hearted men" who devote a "minimized expenditure of time and money and a maximum of interest." He believed it was important to differentiate and individualize each case. "Individual human interest concentrated in a specific Little Brother is called for," he said. "By becoming a Big Brother you signify your desire to improve the condition of some poor unfortunate little fellow who needs your interest and sympathetic advice."

Irv, who remained involved with Big Brothers until his death in 1980 at age 101, recalled what the experience meant to him. "Looking back over the years, back to that contact with little Tom and all of the Little Brothers that followed, I feel that they have given me more than I have given them. They have given me added faith in myself. They have given me the greatest experience of my life."[7]

The Philosophy Spreads

The Big Brothers' philosophy continued to spread throughout the country. As the movement grew, less emphasis was placed on juvenile court cases and it shifted toward preventing and keeping children from getting into trouble.

Big Brothers Big Sisters of America today serves more than 100,000 children a year, enabling them to develop into normal, emotionally stable adults. Why has Big Brothers Big Sisters flourished for more than

90 years? Why does it continue to be one of the most admired social-service organizations in America? Possibly because it seeks to satisfy the basic need that occurs anew with each generation—the need that many children have for an older friend.

"The whole idea behind Big Brothers is to help prevent boys in fatherless homes from getting into trouble, to help them reach their highest physical and emotional development, and to provide an opportunity for compassionate men to make a personal investment of themselves and their futures through the boys," said Irvin Westheimer. Those words were written many years ago, but they continue to describe a pressing, urgent need today and no doubt, tomorrow.

Big Brothers Big Sisters Programs Today

Although some policies guiding each of the Big Brothers Big Sisters agencies differ, their broad mission is the same—to promote and enhance the self-confidence and overall well-being of young people. The principal service of Big Brothers Big Sisters agencies is to provide positive caring adults for children from primarily single-parent families. The service is based upon the premise that when children are affected by a lack of guidance and support due to parental absence or limitation and environmental or situational stresses, youngsters are often deterred from reaching their full potential and may engage in antisocial behavior.

Through one-on-one relationships between youths and positive adults, long-term friendships help youth in the community develop personal responsibility to better face the challenges of the future.

Agencies match young persons with interested adult volunteers who serve as positive role models, mentors, and friends. Matches spend an average of three to four hours per week in shared activities for a minimum of one year. Many relationships last in some form well beyond this requirement.

Mentoring[8]

The word *mentor* originated thousands of years ago in Greek mythology, in the tale of Odysseus. When Odysseus was away from home for many years, he encouraged and entrusted his son, Telemachus, to his friend and adviser, Mentor. While Odysseus was gone, Mentor served as guardian, teacher, and father figure to his young protégé. Mentor means "steadfast" or "enduring." In Western thought mentor has come to be synonymous with anyone who is a wise teacher, guide, and friend.

Mentoring is a one-to-one relationship through which an adult fosters the development of character and competence in a young person. The emphasis is on experiences between two people and the development of the relationship over time. In a one-to-one relationship, the youth is given undivided attention. The focus is on the child and his or her thoughts, feelings, and dreams. This develops the child's sense of importance, self-esteem, and competence.

Mentoring is a relationship that occurs over time. As young people grow, significant experiences shape their lives. Mentoring is not a one-time, life-changing event. Rather, it is an ongoing series of small successes. Through a mentor, a youth may enjoy some adventurous and memorable times, but the real impact comes from the consistent and ongoing relationship building. Mentoring is about consistency and longevity that can be counted on; it is about taking time and being there.

Mentors can be significant, positive influences in the lives of children struggling to know themselves. Mentors can be friends, advocates, and role models. An advocate is one who is willing and active in efforts to further another person's interests. A role model is one who provides a concrete image of possibilities through the example of his or her own actions and life experiences. Role models not only offer example, they also guide and support young people. The mentor's implicit message is: "I will help you be whomever you want to be."

Why Mentoring?

For the mentor, the desire that one's work and influence "live on" is an important life goal. The nurturing and influencing of young adults and the facilitation of their efforts to form and live out their hopes and wishes can fulfill the generative needs of the mentor.

Among the strongest and most compelling reasons for serving as a mentor may be the desire to fulfill one's own need to contribute to the growth, development, and fulfillment of someone else. The act of mentoring allows the mentor to repay, in some measure, the intrinsic benefits derived over a lifetime.

Mentoring is an attractive, effective means of reconnecting adults and children. The Big Brothers Big Sisters programs ask volunteers to focus their mentoring efforts on connecting with just one child, rather than imposing the overwhelming concept of "saving the world." Big Brothers Big Sisters mentoring is a personal, direct way of making an impact.

Mentoring allows individuals to give in a way that is most comfortable for them and does not require specialized skills. One long-time Big Brother volunteer commented that, "To be a Big Brother, you don't have to be a teacher, a child-care expert, or have special talents. You don't have to be a perfect person. The important thing is if you're holding down a job, basically meeting your responsibilities in life, and care about kids."

Positive Adult Male Friendships

"The only decision for us to make is whether boys will define

their masculinity with the help and guidance of strong fathers

and other adults, or whether they will define it by themselves,

perhaps with the help of MTV, or their peers in schools, or gangs

of boys on the street who will be quite ready to tell them—espe-

cially if no one else does—what it means to be a real man."

David Blankenhorn ("Fathers: New Old & Unnecessary,"
Washington Post, *January 30, 1992)*

=◉= =◉= =◉=

Big Impact:
Mike Edwards and Chris Thomas

Big Brothers Big Sisters of Greater Memphis, Tennessee

Chris Thomas was just eight years old in 1972 when he lost most of the men in his family—both of his grandfathers and his great-grandfather. Chris's father had left the family when he was very young, and his mother was working hard—usually at two to three jobs just to keep things afloat. The result was a boy who did not have any men to talk to, learn from, or pal around with.

Chris's mom, Diane, knew Chris might benefit from having a male influence, so she got him into the Big Brothers Big Sisters program of Greater Memphis, Tennessee. Chris was 11 years old when, in 1975, he was matched with Mike Edwards, an 18-year-old freshman at Rhodes College. Mike had become a Big Brother along with three other men in his college fraternity.

Chris was a little intimidated by Mike when they first met, probably because Mike stands six feet six inches tall. The intimidation wore off quickly. Mike remembers that Chris barely said two words the first time they went out for a ride, but according to Mike, "That was the only time he was speechless."

Chris and Mike spent a lot of time on campus, hanging out in the dorms or playing in the nearby park. Mike played football, and Chris used to come to his football games and practices. Chris would walk the sidelines and be the ballboy, which "made me feel really important. When your dad walks out on you, it does something to your self-esteem."[1]

Chris often went to Mike's parents' house for the weekend, where they would do yardwork and go to high school football games. Mike's parents treated Chris just like one of the family.

After high school, Chris worked for a couple of years and got married in 1984. Mike was the best man at his wedding. Chris went on to graduate from Memphis State in December, 1987, with a marketing degree. He got a job working in sales and decided to run for school board at the young age of 26. Chris won, beating a 12-year incumbent in the process. Mike was the treasurer in his school board campaign. Chris is currently a Probate Court Clerk, an elected position that he has won three times. Mike is now a president with First Tennessee Bank. Both are married and have three children.

Chris believes Mike played an important part in his development. "Mike gave me someone to talk to, kid around with; he provided direction in my life. Being around him when he was in college definitely gave me a desire to continue my schooling. Other than my mother and other female family members, Mike Edwards stands out as having had the most influence on me."

Mike believes that he has gotten just as much out of his relationship with Chris. "Each of us led the relationship at different times. Sometimes one of us needed the relationship more. I am not always the Big Brother in this relationship. Sometimes Chris is." Chris and Mike are still in touch. They get together once a month and talk on the phone frequently.

Chris believes strongly that children need support from their community. "Kids need someone other than what's on television. They need someone here face-to-face, someone they can talk to, someone who will invest time in them. Mike has helped me become a leader in this community. When I think back on being a Little Brother at age 11 and how I turned out today, I am very proud. But we have too many people taking from the community instead of giving back. Here in Tennessee it costs $35,000 a year to incarcerate a juvenile. That's ten times what kids get in the school system. But Big Brothers helps counteract that. Being a Big Brother is like investing in the community."

Mike Edwards thinks it is important for men to understand how being a Big Brother is different from other volunteer experiences. His advice to men who are thinking of becoming Bigs is, "Don't go in and think this is charity work, because it can mean much more to you. Don't just do it for them. Do it for yourself. Yes, you must want to do something good for someone else, but if you stay committed, you're doing something good for yourself. It's not an overnight cure for what ails us in America. But it's one small relationship at a time that helps to work miracles."

Mike Edwards and Chris Thomas—one small relationship, one Big Impact.

Male Role Models

Many single-parent households headed by women raise healthy, well-adjusted boys. More often than not, however, when we look at boys who have succeeded, from single- or two-parent families, we find that they have been supported by a number of people, including male role models. The nuclear family alone, no matter what its makeup, cannot always provide the support that is necessary for a boy to grow up. In families where there are no men present, boys often lack a sense of discipline and direction. Without male role models, boys feel lost. And when they feel lost, they seek other ways to find a purpose and a mission in life. In this chapter, we look at some of the needs and issues boys have, and why men should and must play critical roles in the development of boys.

The Road to Manhood

To meet the challenges of growing up in society today, boys need guidance along the road to manhood. Much of that direction is provided by a boy's mother; however, there are times when a mother's words have very little influence. For single mothers, this poses a difficult challenge. A boy growing up without a father may love his mother, but he will probably feel uncomfortable talking with a woman about his masculinity, especially as he reaches the teenage years. He may feel that a woman cannot understand his need to express his manhood. Mothers are not equipped to teach their sons everything they need to know about becoming men. Rather, boys learn how to become men from their fathers and from father figures. Mothers can nurture, teach, discipline, and provide financially for their sons, but they are unable to model male behavior.

Growing up is no easy task for boys, especially if there are no other men around. As David Popenoe, author of *Life Without Father*, points out, "For the lack of male role models, father-deprived children of each sex are at a marked disadvantage in human relationships. . . Making the shift from boyhood to constructive manhood is one of life's most difficult transitions, especially since boys as they grow up must break away from the comforting female arena of their mothers."[2]

Mitch McMurray, a former Little Brother and current Big Brother in Miami, Florida believes it essential to have men involved in a boy's life. "You can have a great mom, but there comes a point in a boy's life when he doesn't have a clue about what it means to grow up. And it is hard for a mother to convey that. It is what attracts boys to drugs, gangs, and getting involved with girls too early in their lives. Just about every kind of negative activity a boy gets involved in, he is driven to by a void in his life, by not having a dad in his life. And unless he has a relationship with a coach, a Boy Scout leader, or a Big Brother—someone who takes an active and personal interest in him because of who he is and for no other reason—then he is not going to have that positive influence that allows him to change from being a boy to a man. And sooner or later, whether he's a good student or bad, he's going to suffer negative consequences from not having that model, from not having somebody that he can look to and see that there is life after childhood."

To grow into a healthy, well-adjusted adult, a boy must separate from his mother at some point. Part of this process involves a boy seeking out other males with whom he might proudly identify. Throughout a boy's growing years, he will continue to look toward other men to guide and reinforce his own masculine development. When a boy does not have any men to identify with, as is so often the case in fatherless homes and communities, he must make up his own idea of what being a man means. Many boys naturally turn to the male images that they see on television. Unfortunately, many of these men are not promoting the values we want to instill in boys. Even worse, these men often promote violence and have led less than model lives themselves.[3]

Other boys look to the few available men in their community, some of whom are gang leaders or criminals. Boys mistake anger and aggression as representative of what manhood means. Without men around as role models, adolescent boys create their own rites of passage. In neighborhoods where there are few fathers, boys are prime candidates for recruitment by the gangs. When there are no older male authority figures present, the void of leadership and support that many boys need will be filled elsewhere.

Social Forces

The adolescent years create major social havoc for boys. As a boy turns 12 or 13, or even younger these days, he suddenly awakens to a brand new world around him, as though his eyes were opening for the first time. The new world is populated by age-mates who scare him out of his wits. His greatest anxiety, far exceeding the fear of death, is the possibility of humiliation or rejection by his peers. This ultimate danger lurks in the background for years, motivating the boy to do things that make absolutely no sense to the adults who watch. It is impossible to comprehend the adolescent mind without understanding the terror of the peer group. Boys are under a lot of pressure to conform to others' ideas of manhood. They need help understanding that being a man is not about hurting others. They also need to learn that it is perfectly appropriate to show emotion and discuss feelings.

Social dominance comes in many forms. Boys derive power from physical attractiveness, but also from athletic accomplishment, from wanting to own beautiful cars and from learning to be cool under pressure. Typically, power games are quite physical for adolescent males. That is why boys are often nervous wrecks on the first day of school, before the team plays its initial game or any other time when their power base is on the line. The raw nerve is not really dominance, but self-esteem. One's sense of worth is dependent upon peer acceptance, which is why boys' peers hold such enormous influence over them. If a boy is mocked, disrespected, ridiculed, and excluded, he is stripped of his power and his delicate ego is torn to shreds.

Through their teenage years, boys continue to lay the groundwork for who they will be as adults. They look to other men to model themselves after and will begin to develop important and often intense relationships with male adults. The men boys choose to identify with directly impact who they will become in the future

What Boys Need

In his book *The Vulnerable Child,* Richard Weissbourd discusses the conditions that all children need in order to prosper. "All children should have a continuous relationship with a consistently attentive and caring adult who treats them as special, who is able to stimulate and engage, who provides appropriate responsibilities and challenges, who passes on important social and moral expectations. Some strong friendships and the affirmation and affection of community adults are often critical to children, especially those who are deprived of the consistent presence of a parent or guardian."[4]

We constantly hear that children need to have significant relationships with adults. For boys without fathers, this means having a friendship with at least one supportive adult male.

Boys Need Anchors

Many boys in single-parent families frequently travel through different family arrangements. It is not uncommon for boys in Big Brothers Big Sisters programs to move many times throughout a match. Each time children move during adolescence, their chances of dropping out of school rise dramatically. Thus it is extremely important for boys to have stable forces in their lives. Boys need anchors—adults outside their families who are caring and attentive over time. Anchors provide a sense of consistency for boys when there is little they can count on regularly.

Boys Need to Channel Their Energy

Boys can have boundless energy. In fatherless homes and communities, physically active boys do not have male mentors to teach them how to channel and contain their aggressive energy in socially acceptable ways—through sports, physical work, and other energetic activities. Their aggressive energy can become useless or destructive if left unchanneled.

Most boys simply need men with whom to engage in activities. While many mothers eagerly engage in activities with their sons, several would prefer that their sons have a male friend. Curt Porteus, a former Little Brother now living in Bozeman, Montana, recalls how important having a male friend like his Big Brother, Les, was to him. "I mainly needed someone to take me out and do activities that my mother could not do. We went camping, hiking, backpacking, and did a lot of other activities. I needed to do them on a consistent basis, and Les always made himself available to me, much to my benefit."

Boys Need a Male Support System

Boys need adult men in the community who can serve in many capacities. They need men who can spot problems, provide opportunities for success, and most importantly, men who will simply listen. An adult male can provide the kind of steady encouragement and recognition that directly impact a boy's basic confidence and trust. For boys who have never had a positive connection with their fathers, adult men can provide a kind of second chance, an opportunity for boys to internalize the confident expectations of an adult other than a parent. Boys need adult men whom they admire and who have some capacity to mirror them, to reflect who they are.

To a boy, male influence is just as important as female influence.

Boys need male influence or they will have a difficult time assimilating with whatever male groups they join. We often hear from boys that, "Sometimes to hear it from a guy carries more weight." Boys especially learn how to deal with conflict from men. Boys need men to teach them how to deal with anger and conflicts by talking and not using force or violence.

We underestimate the need for boys to have time with adult males, their fathers or others. Recently an Illinois neighborhood was considering setting up a Little League baseball program, but was concerned that the kids would not come. Boys showed up in droves—two hours before the scheduled practice—and hung around after practice. Why? They wanted to be around adult men; they craved adult affirmation.

Boys also have lots of issues and questions growing up. Mothers often hear the phrase, "You just wouldn't understand; you're not a guy." Boys have feelings about all sorts of things: sex, drugs, girls, violence, racism, sexism. Boys often express their problems and concerns differently than girls. They rarely admit and discuss their problems. In the presence of men, boys can discuss personal issues without feeling like the focus is on them.

Boys Need to Learn How to Treat Women

Boys and young men learn from other men how to treat women. They observe how men treat their wives, their daughters, and women in general. Boys are very likely to imitate the behavior they see, which depending on their experiences, can have positive or negative consequences. Men can teach boys how to honor and respect girls and women. Boys observe from men that honor and respect come through caring and empathizing rather than from physical violence. Boys learn how to have healthy relationships and see how win/win scenarios are created. They learn important characteristics like listening and setting and keeping agreements. Without these experiences, boys often derive their views on how to treat women from media.[5]

Boys Need Positive Involvement

Boys need a variety of resources to develop into healthy productive men. Relationships with adult men help boys understand and make sense of who they are, respect others, and believe in themselves.

Young men without fathers rarely have the educational and social opportunities to succeed in today's society and are poorly prepared to contribute as providers, protectors, or mentors to their children. In the absence of paternal support, boys need other adult males to fill the void, or the consequences can be problematic.

While all families need support, women who raise boys alone especially require community support from other caring people. Many of the women, mothers, and guardians whom I interviewed for this book, expressed their frustration over the times their voices had little influence. But as Evelyn Bassoff, author of *Between Mothers and Sons*, advises, "Perhaps the best that mothers can do for their sons when they reject their counsel is to lead them to men who are mature, kind, and nurturing, men who will not take advantage of a boy's vulnerability as he strives to assert his masculine strength, but who will rather help find reasonable ways to express it. No matter how able-bodied and supportive, mothers simply cannot teach their sons what they need to know in order to become men."[6]

Our pre-adolescent and adolescent boys face tremendous challenges growing up. They are faced with choices and decisions at every turn. The adult community has often responded by telling youth what not to do. Saying no to drugs, smoking, and alcohol have done little to stop the increase in drug use, teen pregnancy, teen drinking and smoking, AIDS, dangerous driving, and violence in our society. It is simply not effective to moralize against something unless you provide something for which to say "yes." Boys need to learn what is possible and available for them in which to become positively involved.

One of the most effective ways to support boys is through friendships with positive adult men.

chapter

3

The Men of Big Brothers

"Seek always to do some good, somewhere. Every man has to

seek his own way to realize his true worth. You must give time

to your fellow man. For remember, you don't live in a world all

your own. Your brothers are here too."

Albert Schweitzer

≥◎≤ ≥◎≤ ≥◎≤

Big Impact: Craig Porzondek

Big Brothers Big Sisters
of Otsego County, Gaylord, Michigan

Craig Porzondek can say without hesitation that Big Brothers Big Sisters has been a major influence throughout his life. When he was 11 years old and in the fifth grade, Craig's parents divorced, leaving a big void in his life. Craig's father moved more than 200 miles away to Detroit, while Craig moved with his family to Gaylord, Michigan. Craig had an uncle who helped fill the gap, but he also lived far away.

The divorce hit Craig hard. He often did not want to go to school and frequently was sick. Starting at a new school at that age was also difficult for Craig, and he found it hard to make new friends.

At the time Craig's mother, Lori Parshall, was on the board of the Big Brothers Big Sisters program in Otsego County. Sensing that her own son might benefit from the friendship of an adult male, Lori asked Craig one day if he would be interested in having a Big Brother. Craig said he was open to having a Big Brother, but he did not really understand what it was all about.

When Craig was matched with Gary, he said he was "just like my uncle. Gary was into sports, didn't drink or smoke, and was always telling me how important it was to get good grades." Craig believed it was important to have a man in his life, someone who would play sports with him and kid around with him in a male bonding way. What often stood out for Craig was that he knew when he was bored or feeling empty inside, he could always call Gary and say, "Hey, what are you doing? Do you want to get together?"

Having a Big Brother kept Craig from going downhill at a critical time. "I probably blocked out a lot of what happened during those years, but one of the good things I do remember is my Big Brother. I didn't want to let him down. If you don't have anybody to let down, then who cares if you skip school?

*Everything I remember about the time Gary and I spent togeth-
er was positive. You name it, we did it—bow hunting, sailing,
backpacking, baseball, basketball, tennis. It fulfilled something
in a very dark period in my life. Before the divorce, I was one
of the top students, but when I first was matched with Gary I
wasn't even going to school much. After spending time with
Gary, I slowly started to come back. His encouragement and
words like, 'You're doing a good job, keep at it,' really helped
with my self-esteem."*

Craig and Gary were matched for over three years until
Craig was in the tenth grade. Craig went on to finish fortieth out
of 200 students in his class and made the National Honor
Society. He also was one of the top players on the tennis and soccer teams. After high school, Craig went back and forth between
college and the army. He was married in 1988 and also had a
daughter. Both Craig and his wife Susan attended Lake Superior
State. In 1992 Craig graduated with a bachelor's degree and a
3.69 average; he now works in sales in Gaylord, Michigan. In
1994 Craig joined the board of Big Brothers Big Sisters and soon
after became a Big Brother because he "wanted to return the
favor." Craig's Little Brother is John Davis, who was ten years old
at the time they were matched back in the winter of 1994. Craig
and John share many of the same interests, like camping, fishing,
skiing, soccer, and eating.

Craig tries to apply the same principles that his Big Brother
did for him. "What's made the relationship stronger for us is we've
just set aside the connotation about being a Little Brother. John's
not just a boy in a program, he's a member of my family." Craig
knows his role is to be there and encourage John, and he often
goes to watch John's games. Craig tries to set an example of what
it means to be responsible, and he hopes John will see how a
good family relationship works." John's mother has already seen
an improvement in his attitude and his grades. For Craig, having a Little Brother "makes me feel like a kid again. It makes me
feel like my life really has meaning and purpose."

Craig believes having a Big Brother fills an important void
in a boy's life. "Whether you don't have a father or lost a father,
that relationship is always missing. And no matter how old you
are, anything you have, as little as it may be, is going to mean
the world to any kid."

Craig believes more than ever that Big Brothers Big Sisters plays an important role in society. "Today, with all the divorces, society concentrates on the problems of the single-parent family and the lack of control over kids. This is a program that can make a difference. It can turn a kid around."[1] Craig strongly believes that, "Dollar for dollar, Big Brothers is your best investment." For Craig, Big Brothers Big Sisters has more than paid his investment in the program. Craig Porzondek: Little Brother, Big Brother...Big Impact.

≥◎≤ ≥◎≤ ≥◎≤

Give and Take

Men volunteer for a number of different reasons, most notably the desire to help others. Along the way, men learn that by helping others, they are also doing something good for themselves. Some people are uncomfortable with this notion. They see volunteering only as a means of giving.

Susan Ellis, president of Energize Inc., an international consulting and training firm specializing in volunteering, suggests we would all benefit by looking at the experience from a different perspective. "Instead of considering volunteering as something you do for people who are not as fortunate as yourself, begin to think of it as an *exchange,*" she suggests. When volunteers can see the benefits to both the recipient and themselves, they are likely to have a stronger commitment to volunteering. This viewpoint also benefits the self-confidence of recipients, because they are not looked upon as "charity" cases.

This refined definition exemplifies the Big Brother experience for men. While men become Big Brothers to help boys in single-parent families, they often discover that they are receiving as much, if not more, than they are giving. They learn that Little Brothers, no matter what their circumstances, have many gifts to share. In this sense, most men do not look at being a Big Brother as a volunteer experience, but rather an exchange of caring and friendship.

In this chapter, we look at the types of men who become Big Brothers. We also look at what Big Brothers think it takes to be a Big Brother. Finally, we explore why men decide to become Big Brothers and look at some motivational factors sustaining them.

Who Are the Big Brothers?

The term "Big Brother" can conjure up a variety of stereotypical images. Some think Big Brothers are "mostly young men," or "only single men," or "people who don't work for pay," or "only athletic men," or "the wealthy." The reality of who volunteers may surprise you. Each year Big Brothers Big Sisters of America gathers some revealing data from agencies about who volunteers to be Big Brothers. While the numbers go up and down somewhat each time a survey is made, results show that a diverse mix of men become Big Brothers.

Big Brothers come from many different careers. Nearly half are employed at the professional level, with professional and technical workers accounting for 34 percent and administrators and managers making up 15 percent of Big Brothers. More than 12 percent are students. Nearly 9 percent work in sales, and more than 6 percent work in a service capacity. The remainder work in craft, labor, operator, or clerical positions, and about 2 percent of Big Brothers are retired.

The majority of Big Brothers have a college education. More than 56 percent have received an associate's degree or higher. Nearly 20 percent have completed some college, and more than 17 percent of Big Brothers have received a high school, technical degree, or less.

Volunteering to be a Big Brother is not for single men only. While slightly more than half of Big Brothers are single (52 percent), another 38 percent are married. The remaining are either divorced, living with someone, separated, or widowed.

The ages of Big Brothers provide some surprises, too. Thirty-seven percent of Big Brothers are ages 20 to 29. Another 37 percent are ages 30 to 39. And nearly 23 percent of male Big Brother volunteers are age 40 and over.[2]

Unfortunately, race is one of the few categories where there is a noticeable distinction. Eighty-four percent of Big Brothers are white, while over 10 percent are black. About 3 percent are Hispanic, and the remainder are Asian, Pacific Islander, or Native American. There is a large disparity between the number of minority volunteers and minority Little Brothers, matched and unmatched. There are about three times as many minority children as there are volunteers to be matched. The recruitment of minority volunteers has been and continues to be an area of great concern for Big Brothers Big Sisters agencies around the country. While cross-racial matches are just as likely to be successful as same-race matches, Big Brothers Big Sisters would like to offer children the opportunity to have a same race match. Volunteer recruitment efforts targeted to minority populations have been an ongoing priority for agencies.

In many ways, statistics show us that there is no single clear "profile" of the American Big Brother volunteer. Big Brothers can live anywhere, be of any income level, of any age, race, or background. Big Brothers are people who are married and single, employed and retired, students and parents. What distinguishes them from other people more than age, education, marital status, or race is that Big Brothers are all committed, caring people, who enjoy giving and receiving.

What Does It Take to Be a Big Brother?

As they consider the possibility of volunteering to be a Big Brother, most men naturally ask, "What qualities do I need to have and what is required of me?" Again, misconceptions abound about the most important qualities men need to have. First and foremost, a man should want to contribute to the development of a boy and be able to share what he has learned in his life experiences. He should be willing to find reward in service to someone who can benefit from his assistance. He should be able to be supportive and helpful without being overbearing. And, a Big Brother needs to be patient and tolerant when working with someone young.

Time

A Big Brother typically spends three to four hours a week with a Little Brother and also maintains weekly telephone contact. At first glance, prospective volunteers see this as a huge time commitment. But when they look at how their time is currently spent, it often is not difficult to find a couple of hours in their schedules. Most Big Brothers do not look at the time commitment as having to plan an *extra* three or four hours into their schedule. Many successfully incorporate their Little Brothers into activities they already do, such as projects around the house or visiting friends and family.

Time flexibility is one of the most important features to men who volunteer as Big Brothers. Most volunteer experiences require commitment to specific dates and times. Comparatively, Big Brothers are free to schedule their time with a Little Brother when it is convenient for both of them. While many Big Brothers see their Little Brothers on weekends, it is not uncommon to see a Little Brother during the week.

Some Big Brothers have their Little Brothers over for dinner, to do homework, or just to hang out, while other Big Brothers take their Littles to a game or to the gym.

Commitment

A Big Brother must be able to commit to at least one year in many Big Brothers Big Sisters programs, with some programs requiring an 18-month to two-year minimum. The commitment is important for several reasons. Many of the Little Brothers have had someone significant suddenly leave them, thus it is critical to provide some consistency in their lives. Little Brothers need to sense that they can count on their Big Brothers. The commitment is also significant for men. A lot of men have a fear of commitment, of being tied to something for too long. Volunteering often helps men address that fear. Some people view the word commitment negatively, connecting it with something they "have" to do. But most Big Brothers discover that a relationship with a Little Brother is much different than that.

Jeff Venable, a Big Brother in Modesto, California, remembers the thought process he went through when he first became a Big Brother. "I thought it was going to be a much bigger commitment. When I initially thought about the time commitment with the work I was doing, I didn't know if I could do it. But once I got into it, I didn't think of it as a 'commitment' anymore, because I enjoyed doing it and looked forward to it, probably more than anything else I was doing. You do have to have the commitment to follow through. There may be times when you're just not as into it, but when you do it, you end up having a great time. When I started out I wondered how I would have the time. But as I got into it, I started realizing that this was my time to kick back and have fun. I stopped looking at it as something that I had to work into my schedule. And who better to do that with than someone who was an expert at having fun?"

Honoring the commitment to a Little Brother is essential for both Big and Little Brothers. When Big Brothers keep their commitments, they often look at their match as something to look forward to, rather than as a weekly task to be completed.

Openness and Honesty

A Big Brother needs to be open and honest with a Little Brother, which means letting a Little Brother see him for the person he is. It means being able to talk about and translate personal life experiences, good and bad. By being open and honest, a Big Brother encourages his Little Brother to do the same. The more a Little Brother sees his Big Brother being honest with him, the more a Little Brother feels worthy of that honesty and will often reciprocate. Most children are smarter than we give them credit for. They can see through us and know when we are less than honest.

Jeff Venable also has this sound advice for prospective volunteers. "Do not underestimate your own abilities and the gifts that are within you, because it's who you are that a boy desperately needs and wants to see—the gifts of openness and honesty and the ability to affirm the worth of a child. It's the kind of worth that comes from showing up every week, being there and spending time talking. Nothing miraculous has to happen on any given day. But something spectacular is happening. It's a huge deal when a man comes to the door just to see a boy."

If a Big Brother can be open and honest with a Little Brother, he will unlock the door to a solid friendship, a friendship based on mutual respect and trust.

Genuine Concern and Caring

It is important for Big Brothers to have a genuine concern for their Little Brothers. Many Big Brothers become involved in their Little's lives and activities, such as school, clubs, or sports. A Big Brother's interest in his Little Brother's activities helps a Little Brother grow to reach his full potential and will also build his self-confidence.

A Big Brother must be able to demonstrate that he cares about his Little Brother. Again, this does not mean a Big Brother needs to go to great lengths or spend lots of money to show that he cares. The best way for a Big Brother to demonstrate care is through regular contact with a Little Brother. If a Little Brother does not hear from his Big Brother for awhile, he may think it is his fault and wonder what he did wrong. Even if a Big Brother cannot schedule a meeting one week, he should call his Little Brother, explain the situation, and reassure him as to why he cannot meet. Most importantly, he should schedule his next meeting or phone call right away. Surprisingly to most men, a phone call can be very significant to a Little Brother. A phone call after school to see how a Little Brother did on a test or how the floor hockey game went shows that a Big Brother really cares.

Participation

Life is about action and participation. The saying, "You get out of it what you put into it," directly applies to how a match will go for a Big Brother. Little Brothers often mirror back the involvement and interest their Big Brothers put into the relationship. The more energy and enthusiasm a Big Brother displays, the more likely he is to get that same energy and enthusiasm back. Little Brothers, often without their Big Brothers knowing it, are carefully observing how their Big Brothers act. They sense whether a Big Brother is ready to have fun or is just passing the time.

It should be noted that participating actively in a match does not mean a Big Brother must spend exorbitant amounts of time planning trips and outings. Participation means taking an active interest in a Little Brother's life. It also means that when a Big Brother gets together with his Little Brother, he is focusing his energy on his Little Brother. A Big Brother may have a lot going on in his life, but a Little Brother needs to know that his time with his Big Brother is *their* time, and no one else's. Participation means choosing activities that require interaction, talking, and sharing between the Big and Little Brother.

By fully participating in his match, a Big Brother will develop a better relationship with his Little Brother and get a lot more out of time spent together.

What Is Not Required of Big Brothers?

Big and Little Brothers are encouraged to plan activities and outings that cost very little or no money at all. A Big Brother is matched with a Little Brother to be his friend and not to spend a lot of money on him. Little Brothers should learn that friendship is not based on money and what is going to be bought for them.

Big Brothers are not required or permitted to discipline their Little Brothers. This is the parent/guardian's responsibility. If a Little Brother's behavior is unacceptable and he has been given the opportunity to correct it, the Big Brother may take his Little Brother home. It is not up to a Big Brother to discipline a Little Brother. A Big Brother should set ground rules between his Little Brother and himself so they have a mutual understanding of what is acceptable and not acceptable.

A Big Brother should also explain what is important to him and what his commitment to his Little Brother is. That means a Big Brother can discuss how he intends to act and why. I often tell Tony how I react in certain situations and why. I tell him that to gain his respect and understanding, I must act as a friend would, not as a parent.

A Big Brother should not become directly involved in a Little Brother's family issues or problems. A Big Brother can be informed and supportive of a Little Brother, but he is not there to solve a Little Brother's family problems. This does not mean he should not establish trust with a Little Brother's parent or guardian, but he should remember that he is there for his Little Brother only. If a Big Brother has a concern about his Little Brother or his Little Brother's family, he should talk to his caseworker. Caseworkers are there specifically to help, listen, and offer suggestions.

The Right Type of Person

It should be noted that all of the qualities listed above are devoid of certain characteristics: what type of car a person drives, what job they work in, and how much money they have. As one Big Brother I interviewed commented, "What is amazing is how simple this process is and that it requires such a tiny commitment of time. One needn't be rich, socially well-positioned, good looking, athletic, or smart. All that's needed is a piece of one's heart and the absolute conviction to show up punctually for every appointment."

Too many men make the mistake of thinking they need to be the "model citizen" to volunteer. They also think they have to have a lot of nice things to impress a Little Brother. One prospective volunteer told me, "I want to volunteer, but I really want to wait until I move to a better place and get a nicer car." The questions I posed back to him were, "What do you think *really* matters to a child? Do you think spending time together or driving in a fancier car would be more important?"

Being a Big Brother can be both satisfying and challenging. It is satisfying because a Big Brother is enhancing a boy's life and helping a Little Brother reach his full potential. It is also challenging because a Big and Little Brother will learn new things together and teach each other new crafts and hobbies. Many prospective volunteers think that they need to have specialized skills to be a Big Brother. As Senator Daniel Coats from Indiana, a Big Brother for more than 25 years, suggests, "What determines whether or not you would make a good Big Brother is by looking at who you are on the inside and not by how society often judges all of us on the outside."

Why Men Become Big Brothers

When we look closer at why men become Big Brothers, we see a collection of different experiences—from childhood through the world of work and adulthood—that result in a strong desire to connect with a boy.

In 1987 19 Big Brothers Big Sisters agencies participated in a study to identify the motivational factors that influenced men to become Big Brother volunteers. The top three motivational factors as rated by Big Brother volunteers were: doing good for others, sharing mutual relationships, and fulfilling an obligation to society. Other motivational factors included the opportunity to teach values and make good use of their time.[3] Many of the men I interviewed volunteered to be a Big Brother because of the uniqueness of the one-to-one relationship.

Doing Good for Others

The first reason a man decides to volunteer as a Big Brother is usually the result of wanting to do good for others, especially as a role model for a young boy. Some volunteers have reacted directly out of concern for the growing number of fatherless boys in their communities. Others believe that they have the ability to share friendship with a boy. By doing so, they have a chance to aid in a boy's growth, and have the satisfaction of making a positive impact on a young man's life.

Often men volunteer because they can relate to what it means to be a boy growing up without any involved adult men. Some volunteers grew up in single-parent situations themselves, while others have experienced other issues facing Little Brothers, such as a parent's death, divorce, or abandonment. These men recognize firsthand the importance of having a male influence. Many of these men were once Little Brothers themselves.

Mike McNabb was a 12-year-old kid in 1972 when his parents divorced. Mike's father lived out of state, so his mother got him involved in the Big Brothers Big Sisters program in St. Paul, Minnesota. Although he was only matched with his Big Brother Jim for a year and a half, the program had a big impact on his life. Mike knew he wanted to get back into the program after he graduated from the University of Minnesota in 1984. Mike saw strong similarities between himself and his Little Brother Greg when they were matched more than six years ago. They talked a lot about the difficulties of growing up without a father figure. Mike believes that, "It's pretty powerful when you have someone you can talk to who can say 'You know, I went through the same thing, and I felt the same things you do, and it's not your fault. You didn't do anything to deserve this or cause this, and you're not alone.'" That positive impact has carried forward, because today Greg is attending Harvard University, and Mike has been president of the board of directors of Big Brothers Big Sisters of Greater St. Paul since 1995.

Sharing Mutual Relationships

Many men become Big Brothers simply because they like being around children. They enjoy both giving to and receiving from children. That means that while they want to play a supportive role for a child, they also know there is a lot to learn from a child. For many men, becoming a Big Brother is a fun way to interact and connect with a child, with the opportunity to develop a long, lasting relationship.

Some men who are fathers themselves want to maintain the connection to kids once their own children are grown. Hugh Anderson said he got interested in the Big Brothers Big Sisters program in Trumball County, Ohio, when he accompanied his boss on camping trips with his boss's Little Brother. "My children are now 26 and 25 and are raised. I love children and wanted to still be involved with them. I found by volunteering for this organization I could still have the delight in seeing children grow up and at the same time help someone."[4]

For other men who do not have children, being a Big Brother is their only opportunity to regularly interact with boys. Briton Bullock got involved as a Big Brother because he had no family of his own, had the time, and enjoyed being around children. Brit, a former Michigan resident, has had ten Little Brothers since 1952. Brit has taken his Little Brothers canoeing, camping, skating, swimming, and skiing. "They loved the activity," he said, "and it was good for me too." Although he is now retired and living in Ocala, Florida, Brit is still in touch with eight of his ten Little Brothers. Brit regularly contacts and visits with them. One of Brit's Little Brothers, Dan Sheko, now 31, has been a Big Brother to Lee Setty for more than ten years in Plano, Texas. A few years ago Dan helped celebrate Brit's 75th birthday by organizing a surprise birthday party for him. Many of Brit's friends and some of his past Little Brothers attended.

Fulfilling an Obligation to Society

A lot of men today are frustrated by the few opportunities they have to act on their social consciences. They feel the need to do some good in the world on a personal level, and often their work does not accommodate that. They choose to volunteer as Big Brothers, because it is one of the few organizations where it is possible to make a direct and personal impact. Volunteering to be a Big Brother is a more satisfying way to contribute than by simply writing a check. As Dan Wright, a Big Brother in Port Charlotte, Florida, says, "There are a lot of worthy organizations out there that you can contribute money to, but not a lot where you get to see the direct results."

Thomas Shadrick got involved because he was getting concerned about the number of kids he saw every day—the ones that kept appearing in his courtroom. As a circuit court judge in Virginia Beach, Virginia, Tom found himself sentencing too many young men to long prison terms in Virginia's correctional system. He felt strongly that he needed to make a personal commitment to help influence the life of one boy and actively recruit others to do the same through Big Brothers Big Sisters of South Hampton Roads.

In February of 1995 Tom was matched with 9-year-old Jeremy, whose father had died when he was just two years old. Jeremy was identified as a special needs child at school with behavioral and academic problems. Since they have been matched, Tom has devoted every Saturday and frequent evenings to Jeremy, engaging in fun, healthy, recreational, and educational activities. Tom offers Jeremy direct help in developing healthy social relationships, personal habits, and motivation for achievement. The result of their time together has improved Jeremy's schoolwork. His fourth grade teacher says, "I have seen Jeremy come from being a sullen and aggressive child to one who makes a valiant effort to succeed in school." For Tom, becoming a Big Brother was important because, "I see too many people pointing fingers at other people in society, so I decided that I needed to be a part of the solution."

Teaching Values

Volunteering is an opportunity to pass on certain values and traditions of being a man, a family person, and a community member. To some Big Brothers, this means showing a Little Brother a good family atmosphere and how to follow rules. Other Big Brothers teach Little Brothers about honesty, the value of money, and the importance of a good education.

Making Good Use of Time

Some Big Brothers find that volunteering is an opportunity to make better use of their time. It is an opportunity to meet new people, see new places, and try new activities. For others, volunteering is a chance to make a direct impact and to feel that they are contributing to society. When volunteers evaluate how they spend their time, they see that they spend a lot of time at work or on other activities that do not bring a lot of personal satisfaction. Being with a Little Brother makes most Big Brothers feel like they have spent their time well. As one Big Brother told me, "You never feel better about yourself than when you have spent time with a child, and when you leave that child is smiling."

The One-on-One Concept

To many Big Brothers, especially those who have volunteered in other organizations, one-on-one mentoring is very different from anything they have ever experienced. Being a Big Brother stands out because it gives men a specific sense of community and responsibility, and they get to see the impact of a one-on-one relationship.

Jeff Lambrecht, a Big Brother with Big Brothers Big Sisters of Metropolitan Detroit, put it simply, "This isn't like any volunteer work you've done in the past. I don't care what you've done, what board you've served on, or what soup kitchen you've served at, or anything else. This volunteer work is different, and it's different because it's got flexible time and you get to do things you enjoy. That's the secret, do things you enjoy doing anyway, and introduce your Little Brother or Sister to it. And then you'll have fun. It's more fun than anything I've ever done. And, it's got the added bonus of being the most satisfying because you can see the little changes along the way, and then you know you're making a difference."

chapter

4

Little Brothers

"Big Brothers Big Sisters was started over 90 years ago, and today, there is increasing evidence that no other program for troubled youth is more effective."

Parade Magazine, *August 6, 1995*

≥⊚← ≥⊚← ≥⊚←

Big Impact:
A Special Tribute to Paul and Nathan[1]

Big Brothers of Rhode Island

Paul Oberg was driving to work one day in 1978 when he heard an advertisement for Big Brothers. He had coached CYO baseball and basketball before but had never really had any lengthy conversations with kids. So when Paul got to his office, he decided to call Big Brothers of Rhode Island. After he was approved by the agency, director Val Sinesi told Paul he had a match for him—Nathan. There was just one problem—Nathan had a serious medical condition. Just nine years old, Nathan underwent dialysis treatment for four hours at a time, three days a week, traveling back and forth by bus each time. Nathan's kidneys had begun failing after he was just one year old. That did not deter Paul; he agreed to the match.

On their first outing, Paul and Nathan went out for Chinese food. They immediately found they had a lot in common. Nathan's birthday was May 1; Paul's May 2. They both used their middle name as their first name—Paul was C. Paul Oberg, and Nathan was J. Nathan Baker. They both seemed excited by their new friendship.

Paul decided to learn more about Nathan's life and his condition. Nate, as Paul called him, had seen more than his share of difficulties. His parents divorced when he was very young, leaving him to live with his mother, Betty, and sister, Natalie. The family struggled financially for a bit, while Betty went to college to get a psychology degree. When he was four Nathan had a kidney transplant. After the operation he was given strong drugs to counteract the effects of the new organ. The kidney took hold for only five years until it was removed when he was nine. Nathan was also in counseling to help him deal with the stress of his condition. He felt very different from other kids, because he did not have much of a life. Nathan would never grow to be taller than 4 feet, 11 inches, and his condition often left him exhausted and unable to walk. As a result, he did not have many close friends.

His mom realized Nathan might benefit from a male role model, and so she had called Big Brothers.

Paul believed Nate just needed someone to take him away from his day-to-day environment. "I saw my role as being his best friend outside of the family. I wanted to give to him and do for him what he couldn't do in his normal life. I wanted to be the guy he could call up and talk to about anything."

And talk they did. Paul is a management consultant who frequently travels. He would usually call Nathan during the week to discuss their upcoming Saturday get-togethers. They would often talk for hours at a time. Paul would tell Nathan all about his work consulting to consumer products companies. He would send Nathan product samples, as well as souvenirs from all the cities he visited.

When Saturdays came Paul and Nathan did all sorts of activities. They would go to sporting events, car shows, the circus. Paul took him sailing on his boat and let him steer. When Nathan was ten, Paul arranged for him to go to Washington, DC with him. Paul had a friend who worked in the White House who arranged a special tour for them. The trip was Nathan's first on an airplane and his first stay in a hotel. Paul remembers walking around carrying Nathan on his shoulders. Paul would have to arrange for dialysis wherever they went, and Nathan would often get tired. But they went everywhere, from the Smithsonian, to the Capitol, to the Tomb of the Unknown Soldier. Nathan came home with a lot of special memories.

Paul was becoming an important person in Nate's life, but Nate would also be there for Paul at a critical time in Paul's life. Soon after becoming a Big Brother, Paul went through a difficult divorce. Nate was there to console him. "Nathan was my reason to come home," Paul says. "I had two things to latch onto—my job and Nate. He became a priority along with my work. I felt not wanted and needed myself, but Nate helped me get through that."

When Paul was considering remarrying a few years later, his fiancee, Betsey, knew she would have to pass the Nate test. "More than anything, I was concerned about Nate liking me, because I knew how close he and Paul were. If Nate didn't like me, I'm not sure what would have happened," Betsey recalls. Fortunately, they hit it off well and Nate, at 13 years old, was the best man at Paul's wedding in 1982. Paul remembers picking

Nate up at the hospital the day of the wedding. He reminded Nate that, even though Paul was married, Nate would never be alone. "I told him he always had a place in my life. I also encouraged him to think about his own life, and the possibility of going to high school and beyond."

Nate liked Betsey, and he made sure to watch out for Paul's best interests. When Paul would travel for work, Nate would often call Betsey and ask her out to lunch, dinner, or a movie. Nate became a part of their family. If Nate did something for Paul, he would do something for Betsey. When he arranged to have friends get Whitney Houston tickets for Paul, he made sure to get Huey Lewis tickets for Betsey.

Paul and Nate continued to see each other regularly, while Nate attended high school in Pawtucket. One day in the spring of 1987, Nate called Paul with some important news—he had met a girl, Melissa, whom he really liked. Paul and Betsey went out with Nathan and Melissa on their first dinner date. Paul was soon to be a sounding board for relationship advice. He would also be a sounding board to Betty, who would talk to him about Nate's condition, but also express her gratitude for Paul's involvement. One of Paul's proudest days was when Nate graduated high school with his class. He and Betsey, Melissa, Nate, and Betty all went out to dinner afterward.

By 1990 Nate's condition began to worsen. The dialysis treatments he was receiving were no longer working, because there were no longer any places on his body to make the connections to transfer the needed blood. Nate began a new treatment that required inserting a tube into his body to transfer and drain fluids from his body. The new method required six-hour treatments, which could be done while he was sleeping, five days a week. They seemed to work. Nate began attending Rhode Island College.

In 1991 Nate and Melissa became engaged, exactly four years to the day of their first date, and they got an apartment together. Unfortunately, they could not get officially married, because it would jeopardize the government benefits Nate was receiving for his medical bills.

Not long after the engagement, Nate began to suffer a lot of pain again, both physically and emotionally. He felt ill often. Paul frequently spent many hours in the hospital with him, where the staff started referring to him as Nate's uncle. Nate's mother Betty, who had moved to Kentucky, died suddenly after suffering a stroke in 1992. Paul remembers that after Betty died Nate hugged him for the first time.

Nate began talking to Paul about doing something positive together, perhaps speaking on behalf of Big Brothers to recruit more volunteers. They would share the experiences of their 14 years together. The agency liked the idea.

Unfortunately Nate never got his chance. In October of 1992 Nate went into the hospital with a lot of pain and was not doing well. Paul sat with him for over two hours. They talked about the things they were going to do, and how much fun speaking for Big Brothers was going to be. Nathan improved after that for a day, enough so that Paul thought he could go on a one-day business trip. While in Houston Paul received a call at four in the morning from Betsey: Nate had taken a turn for the worse. He died two hours later, with Melissa by his side. The plane ride home was "the longest I had ever taken. I felt so alone," recalled Paul. The last thing he did for Nate was to arrange his funeral.

Paul believes that his time with Nathan helped make the boy's life a little brighter. "Even when he didn't feel well," said Paul, "he always knew there was something else in life. I think our match gave him the feeling that he could have more of a life. I remember when he started talking about going back to school, to college and thinking about what he wanted to be. He became interested in my work and subjects like math and science. I think he began to hope and developed a new outlook—all of this from a kid who wanted to die at age nine. Nate had more courage than most of us will ever know."

Despite the outcome, Paul never regrets a moment of the time he spent with Nathan. "I would do it all over again," said Paul. Nathan's death made Paul realize what is important in life. The time he spent with Nathan has put a whole new meaning on parenting, especially now that he has two boys of his own.

Nathan had hoped that he and Paul could speak together to promote Big Brothers. He wanted to tell everyone that he and Paul were proof that the program worked.

You never got a chance to say it, but you were right, Nathan. Together, you and Paul made a Big Impact.

A Desperate Need

Kathleen Murphy, executive director of Yavapai Big Brothers Big Sisters in Prescott, Arizona, believes that, "You can change what people say is unchangeable, like the cycle of having many children. One of our former Littles, now 30 years old, had a father who had 18 children." Kathleen also believes that prevention is the key to the program's success. "It's not what you change, it's what doesn't change, because we're a true prevention program. If a kid stays the same and doesn't get worse, that is a wonderful accomplishment. If they don't get in trouble with the law, grades don't go down, girls don't get pregnant, kids stay in school, and don't get involved with gangs, we're successful. We may not be turning around behavior, but truly giving a child something to prevent that behavior." However, with lengthy wait lists, the crisis will continue to grow. "I think people are hungry for something that works. There's a sense that we get now, especially from people in the community, that if we don't find something that works, we'll be in deep trouble for a long time. We should be serving ten times as many kids as we do here," said Kathleen.

The Benefits to Little Brothers

When we look more closely at the day-to-day experiences of Big and Little Brothers, it is possible to discern a range of positive developments linked to the mentoring experience, with important benefits in many areas. This chapter looks at some of the benefits that Little Brothers have derived from their relationships with a Big Brother. The results of my interviews suggest that even though a Big Brother is not solely responsible for a boy's success, the relationship helps provide many essential elements that lead down the pathway to a healthy, productive adulthood. The Abell Foundation in Baltimore, Maryland, reminds us that, "Mentoring isn't a panacea for all the problems facing young people and their families. But through a mentor's sustained caring, interest, and acceptance, mentees begin to think of themselves as worthy of this attention—and may apply their new self-confidence to other relationships and experiences."

Exposure to New People, Places, and Experiences

Dan Shemer, a Big Brother through Jewish Big Brothers Big Sisters League of Baltimore points out, "A Big Brother shows a Little Brother options and choices and that there are decent things happening out there in the world."

Jerry Cleveland, a Big Brother in Verona, Virginia, introduced his Little Brother, Anthony, to farming. Anthony learned how to drive a tractor and operate machinery. This was significant for Anthony because he was the type of child who thought he could not do those things. When Anthony would express his doubt over his ability, Jerry would say, "Well, have you tried before? How do you know unless you try?" Jerry's encouragement to try new experiences like farming helped develop Anthony's confidence.

Another example is the exposure to a college education. Sometimes this exposure has a lasting impact. Meredith Lopes never thought she'd see her grandson, Errol, make it to college. Errol had a difficult childhood to say the least. His mother died when he was six, and he went to live with his grandmother who became his guardian. Errol's father died several years later.

Meredith remembers that after Errol's mom died it was "like he hit a brick wall. He just closed down." When Errol was three or four years old, he was in a gifted children's program. After his mother's death, he was put in a special education class. Errol's doctors said his mind would just shut down on things. According to Meredith, "Errol's attention span was so short that you could go over a homework problem with him and he would look at it, do it, turn the page and go back to it as if he hadn't seen the problem before. It was frustrating because he had a lot of anger inside. He would daydream a lot and have outbursts of anger."

Errol did not have any male influence in his life because Meredith was divorced from his grandfather and his father had never really been in the picture. So Meredith got in touch with the local Big Brothers program in Rhode Island and eventually Errol, at age ten, got matched with Ken, a college student at Brown University. They hit it off immediately.

Errol and Ken went to a lot of Brown sports games. Ken also got Errol interested in soccer and chess. Errol loved to read, so he and Ken spent a lot of time at the Brown bookstore.

The emphasis in this match was not on spending money or even what they did—it was the quality time that they spent together. It did not matter if Ken just brought Errol down to the campus and went bowling, or they went to the movies or played sports.

Meredith believes that Errol opened up to Ken in a way that he could not with her. Ken always talked about the importance of education with Errol. He helped Errol with his self-confidence and low self-esteem. Errol thought that since he was in special education, he must be stupid. Ken realized that Errol was not applying himself, and Ken helped him find some direction. With Ken's influence, Errol's change in attitude in the next couple of years brought him from the low end of the school spectrum to near accelerated level. By the eleventh grade, Errol started tutoring kids in geometry and even received several academic awards. Errol is currently pursuing a degree in anthropology and is planning a trip to Brazil. He also has a summer job mentoring and tutoring younger children.

Meredith says Ken had a huge impact on Errol. "Ken was there at a time when Errol needed him. Ken gave of his time, and it was quality time. Getting involved in the Big Brothers program saved my grandson's life. I don't mean he would have died without the program; I'm sure he probably would have gone the other route because drugs and everything were so available to his friends who are dead from drugs. Errol has friends in jail because of drugs. He has friends who are out there actively using drugs. And I think the Big Brothers showed Errol that there was something else he could do instead of hanging on the street doing and selling drugs. He has often told me, "Nana that could be me. I feel very fortunate that Big Brothers was there. I believe it from the heart if Errol had not gotten involved with Big Brothers and Ken, to see what the college setting was about, it would not have been in his head to go to college. What was important was that Errol knew that this was a special person just for him, which helped his self-confidence and self-worth. Somebody cared enough about him to spend some time. Too much emphasis nowadays is put on material things, but if you can show a kid that he's worth something and that he deserves someone to spend some time with him, that can mean so much. Kids can say a lot, but what they really mean is they want someone to like them for who they are. And I think that's what Big Brothers does."

A Man's Perspective

Boys look to men to help them make sense of the changes they are going through as they progress through adolescence. The Big Brothers I interviewed frequently mentioned that as their relationships developed the topics they discussed with their Little Brothers turned from surface issues like sports to more serious "guy's stuff"— like sex. Big Brothers play a critical role in helping boys filter the various messages they receive and help them make sense of their world in a way that builds self-confidence and social competence. Boys desperately want and need guidance and support to evaluate all the choices available to them.

While mothers and women play a very important role, there are times when they feel limited in their ability to teach boys how to be men.

Portia Wallace, an African-American single mother who is a detective with the county sheriff's police, regularly sees children from single-parent homes come through her department. But when her own son, Johnathan, became a teenager, she started to hear comments from Johnathan like, "You wouldn't understand, you're not a man." Portia became concerned because, "I could tell Johnathan how to be a person, but I couldn't tell him what it was like to be a black man growing up in America, and he needed that." Johnathan had not had any sustained relationships with adult males, having little significant contact with his father or grandfather, which at times left him angry.

Portia felt Johnathan needed to have a relationship with an adult male, so she turned to Big Brothers Big Sisters of Lake County in Gurnee, Illinois. Johnathan and Mark, an African-American in his late 20s, were matched on Christmas eve in 1985. Johnathan was 15 at the time. When they met on that first night, their caseworker asked them all what they wanted. Johnathan replied, "All I want is for him to be my Big Brother."

According to Portia, "It was like a match made in heaven. Within six months, the anger was gone. Mark understood Johnathan's fear and nervous energy as a black boy. He understood his need to be accepted. Mark knew what to do and say." Johnathan did things with Mark that he had previously been afraid to do, like riding the train and in a glass elevator.

Mark proved to Johnathan that he could have a relationship with a significant adult in his life. Through that match, Portia said, "Johnathan realized that anything that happened with his father or grandfather was not his fault."

As a result of Mark and Johnathan's match, Johnathan's relationship with his mother changed. "I didn't get the angry Johnathan anymore. All these minor victories just made my heart leap for joy. It took away a lot of my worries of what he was going to be like at age 16. I felt blessed by Mark's presence. My angry, biting kid was gone. He's 25 now, and he's a barber, going to school. And he's realizing his dream."

The impact the Big Brothers program had on Johnathan has made Portia a strong advocate for Big Brothers Big Sisters. "The program made me feel like someone is really concerned about what my son needed that I couldn't give him." Portia has been a member of the Big Brothers Big Sisters board for over 12 years, and has been a Big Sister for over five years.

Having a Big Brother helps Little Brothers learn how to deal with situations and issues in a more constructive manner. Steve Baker, who was a Little Brother to Dave Dubelle back in 1978, remembers how Dave helped with his attitude. "I had a temper, but Dave helped teach me other ways to deal with anger. I saw what anger can do, because I knew someone who was imprisoned for killing a woman. Dave showed me more constructive ways of dealing with conflict. I'd probably be in prison were it not for Dave." Steve is now working for a company that makes paint for cars, while living in Highland, Michigan.

A Role Model

Little Brothers benefit by having a male influence who models good male behavior. As the late Jerry Cohen of Marblehead, Massachusetts, a Big Brother to Brad Seidel for more than 25 years said, "Sometimes boys are more influenced by an outsider or someone they look up to. A son may just not listen to what his mother says no matter how good the advice. A Big Brother can have an impact because his presence helps influence a boy. It sinks in subtly, but it does sink in." Brad certainly listened to Jerry's words of advice and encouragement over the years. After graduating from high school, Brad joined the Navy for six years and went on to own his own comic books store. And now at age 35 (finally!!), Brad is in his senior year at Babson College in Wellesley, Massachusetts.

Building Self-Worth

Gerry Murphy, the oldest of five children and the only male, became a Little Brother when he was around 11 years old shortly after his parents divorced in 1972. The divorce left Gerry confused, lonely, and angry, which created a distrust of adults. He wondered if this was the way adults were. If so, Gerry did not want any part of it. He had been a good student, but the divorce left Gerry unwilling to do his schoolwork or turn in his assignments. He felt like he needed to take on more responsibility in his home for his mom and four sisters.

When matched with Matt Bradley, Gerry was eager for a new friend but very cautious about liking him for fear he might leave one day. Self-conscious over his situation, Gerry was not comfortable with the fact that he lived in a low-income neighborhood and had to live sparingly. He got over that pretty quickly with Matt, who at the time was an air force pilot stationed in Topeka. Not only was Matt fun to be with, he showed Gerry that he liked him for who he was. "When I was with Matt, it was like a different world. Without saying or doing anything, I was able to sense that none of that mattered to him. He helped me understand a person isn't what their circumstances are, and that it doesn't matter. He taught me that you have the potential and the ability to do and be whatever you want, and that the other stuff doesn't have any bearing on that. That's what the relationship meant to me."

Now Gerry gets along well with his mother and has a much closer relationship with his two youngest sisters. He believes that, "The closeness and trust I developed with Matt, probably helped me share some of the same feelings with my sisters."

Today, Gerry has his own residential remodeling business. He has also been a Big Brother to Jason for more than two years with Big Brothers Big Sisters of Topeka, Kansas. He believes boys greatly benefit from having a Big Brother because, "Young people are generally products of their environment. If they don't have some outside influence to show them an alternative, then there is no alternative. A Big Brother helps a boy see that there are other options. In the end it is up to the Little Brother to decide whether or not to pursue those options, but at least he has been shown what they are."

Building Confidence

Many Little Brothers benefit by the unconditional support given to them by their Big Brothers. Big Brothers encourage their Little Brothers to stretch their belief in themselves, to try things out of their comfort zone. With a Big Brother's support, a Little Brother often will excel in areas that the Little Brother never imagined possible.

Mike Radakovich was always supportive of his Little Brother, Bill. They often went to sporting events at nearby James Madison University. Bill really like James Madison, but when it came time to apply to college, he figured it would be too hard to get accepted there. Mike encouraged Bill to apply anyway, telling him to always go for his dreams. Bill was so excited when he called to tell Mike of his acceptance. Bill is now a junior at James Madison, studying graphic arts. He hopes to do graphic arts in Hollywood one day, again with Mike's encouragement to "shoot for the stars."

Giving Boys Hope

Timothy Daniels had never known his father. He became a Little Brother in the late 1960s when his mom was dying of cancer. At the age of eight, Timothy was matched with Pan Am pilot Otis Young, the first black pilot to fly 747s. Timothy learned a lot about hope from his Big Brother. "The most important thing Otis taught me was that I was only at a starting point in life, and that life could get better," said Timothy.

"Otis told me about the value of education and that it was important to listen to adults," Timothy recalls. With Otis, Timothy learned such things as how to play baseball and fish.

After his mom died, Timothy went to live in Dallas for awhile before coming back to live with his older sister in San Francisco. He lost contact with Otis, who now lives in Maryland, and it took him 15 years to track him down. Timothy and Otis now keep in touch periodically. "Until I contacted him he had no idea what impact he had on my life. I could easily have ended up selling drugs or been in a gang. I also learned it was important, if I became a father, to have a good relationship with my children." And that is why Timothy has a solid bond with his two daughters, ages 14 and 10. But Timothy has taken on more than just the role of a good father. For the past few summers, he has been part of a group that puts on summer basketball camps for underprivileged kids. "We use basketball as the hook to get kids in and let them know that there are other things in life besides gangs, drugs, and truancy. Police and college recruiters come in and speak. Kids leave the camp fully informed about a lot of things. My payback is just to see a kid succeed and help someone else—to keep the cycle going."

"My life could have been very ugly, with my mom dying, not having a dad, and with the environment I lived in and getting shuffled around for awhile. Had it not been for Otis Young, my Big Brother, I probably wouldn't be the person I am today." Timothy now runs a retail store featuring African-American goods in Modesto, California.

Raising Their Own Expectations

Boys are often products of their environments. Parents who have not completed high school or college do not usually place education expectations on their sons. As a result, boys do not place any expectations on themselves. Big Brothers do not place unrealistic expectations, but can successfully help boys "raise the bar" of expectations on themselves to succeed. I consistently tell Tony that he can be whatever he wants to be, and that is entirely up to him.

Having Matt as his Big Brother helped Tom Walsh to raise his expectations of himself. "Without Matt's advice to push myself, I wouldn't have gone to Catholic school for the last six years of junior high and high school. This has shaped my life in a very positive sense. If it hadn't been for Matt's influence, I would not have shot that high on my list of standards. He told me to shoot for the stars. He helped me raise my expectations of myself, and he showed me that there's life outside of where I was living."

From high school Tom went to community college, but Matt told him to "look beyond his means." This encouraged Tom to go to Syracuse University, where he graduated in 1991 with a dual major in economics and psychology. Tom now works as an account executive for Online Business Associates in Stamford, Connecticut.

Tom attributes a lot of his success to Matt. "He taught me that there was more to life than the neighborhood I grew up in, which was often like a war zone. If it hadn't been for Matt's influence I don't think I would have been able to cope through many of my childhood years. Matt helped me be strong and gain confidence."

Last summer, on the twentieth anniversary of their match, Tom decided to make up a plaque for Matt that read,

"Thank you for taking me out on weekends.

Thank you for always being there when I needed you

and for helping me become the man I am.

I don't feel I have ever thanked you enough

for what you have done for over 20 years.

And you have done a lot, whether you realize it or not."

Caring and Compassion

Many of the changes that Big Brothers observe in their Little Brothers are very subtle and gradual. One change is often in Littles' attitudes toward their Big Brothers or friends and families. Jeff Lambrecht remembers when he noticed a change in his Little Brother Jack. Jeff and Jack were playing basketball once, and afterward Jack picked up Jeff's coat for him. "He did something a little courteous that he wasn't doing before. Those are the little things that tell you he is not the same person you first met. It's the subtle signs that show you he is putting a bit more thought into his actions and being more considerate," recalled Jeff. Jeff is also seeing very visible signs of change in Jack. He has gone from a student near failing out of school and getting in trouble to a more well-behaved B student.

In other instances, Little Brothers become advocates for their Big Brothers. Neil Young, a Big Brother to both Eric and Lyle, remembers a time when they supported him when he needed it most. "I had broken off my wedding plans, and they were a great support to me. They decided they should spend the night with me because they didn't want me to be alone. They were like true brothers to me."

Relating to Women and Other Adults

Jimmy Watts, an African-American Big Brother in Jacksonville, Florida, regularly has his little brother, Jammie, spend time at his home. "One of the most important things Jammie has seen is my relationship with my wife. And I now see the way that he treats his girlfriend, and I think he's going to be a good husband and father one day. He even talks of being a Big Brother one day, and that's one of the greatest rewards," says Jimmy.

Breaking Down Barriers

For many Little Brothers, being matched with a Big Brother is often their first consistent exposure to someone of a different race. Ki-Jana Carter, a former Little Brother, remembers how race was never a factor in his relationship with Big Brother Scott Gordon, whom he has known since he was ten years old. "Throughout my family and Scott's family, we never looked at the relationship as a white/black thing. We are Big and Little Brothers. And that's one thing that Big Brothers does for families, it erases all that racial boundary and financial status. We struggled, me and my Mom, and Scott came from a good family, but he treated me the same. Love was the big thing, and that's what it was about. It wasn't about how much money you had or what race you were."[2]

Scott also taught Ki-Jana to have good moral values. Ki-Jana says that, "He didn't sit me down and tell me to do this or that. He just led by example. What made me appreciate him were the little things he did. He taught me about being a good person, that life was more than about athletics." Ki-Jana has not only excelled as a person through his relationship with Scott, his athletic life continues to prosper. Ki-Jana graduated from Penn State with a degree in marketing and was also the Heisman trophy runner-up in 1994. He is now a running back for the Cincinnati Bengals. He and Scott continue to stay in touch to this day, and Ki-Jana continues to support Big Brothers Big Sisters. Last NFL season, he started the "Ki-Jana 300," which represented his season-long quest to seek out adult volunteers for the 300 Tri-State children presently on a waiting list for a Big Brother or Big Sister.

Providing a Sense of Security

Jeff Stanley was matched with Hunt Berryman when he was ten years old through Big Brothers Big Sisters of Polk County, Florida. Jeff said he always felt a bit insecure growing up, but that being around Hunt, "made me feel at ease. I looked up to him and wanted to be like him. But it was always the small things he did that meant more to me. As a result, I felt better about myself."

Although they were only matched for three years, Jeff has stayed in contact with Hunt. After Jeff, now 28, went to college at Stetson University, he began working for Hunt's trucking company. He also was a Big Brother himself until a couple of years ago when his Little Brother moved out of state. "I wanted to give back to someone because of my experiences as a Little. I wanted to expose someone to new things and make them feel better about themselves, like Hunt did for me," said Jeff.

Preparing Boys for the Future

Big Brothers help Little Brothers think through important choices— about school, work, and future. And Big Brothers encourage Little Brothers to reach their full potential.

Shajan Kay owes a lot to Jim Webb and Joey Wauters. When Shajan Kay was just five years old, his parents divorced. After being on the waiting list at Big Brothers Big Sisters of Juneau, Alaska, for more than two years, Shajan was matched with Jim Webb and Joey Wauters as a couples match in 1987. He was 12 years old at the time. According to Shajan, "They were the best thing that ever happened to me."

Although they were matched for several years, Jim and Joey were not sure if they were making a difference. "We didn't know for many years if we were making any impact, and we were. We just didn't get the feedback until years later when Shajan wrote wonderful warm-hearted letters thanking us," recalled Joey. When Shajan became a freshman in high school, he let Jim and Joey know how much their relationship meant to him through a Christmas card. "They pushed me to do well in school. Without them, I would have dropped out around my sophomore year," says Shajan. He was elected twice to offices while in high school, and also participated in the debate teams. These were things that Jim and Joey were pleasantly surprised to see. "When we first met him you could never have imagined it," recalled Joey.

"To me, having a Big Brother and Big Sister meant the difference from living my life as a high school dropout to living the life of a successful college student who will probably go on to a masters program and more," said Shajan. Being matched has, according to Shajan, "given me a sense of my worth as a person and goals for the future. When I first started, I did not feel I had much of a chance of a future, but Jim and Joey encouraged me to dream of such goals as going to college. I believe that I will be successful in whatever I am determined to do." Today, Shajan is attending Oakland University in Rochester, Michigan, where he is a member of the Executive Cabinet of the Oakland University Student Congress.

Giving Life Meaning

In certain cases, the impact on a Little Brother can be dramatic. Bob Mitchell, executive director of Big Brothers Big Sisters of Greater St. Paul, Minnesota, recounts how one story continued when it was expected to have ended. "About eight or nine years ago, one of our caseworkers got a call from a hospital social worker. They had a 12-year-old child who had terminal cancer. He had foster parents who said they were wasting time with him. The social worker asked if we could find him a Big Brother. Sometimes that would be tough given the situation, but as luck would have it, we had a Big Brother who was just coming off of a relationship with a Little Brother. He was also starting medical school, and he agreed to be matched knowing the situation. He helped the child who spent a lot of time in the hospital for chemotherapy. About four months into the relationship, we got a call from the doctor. He told me that the boy had gone into remission, and the only thing they could find was that this Big Brother relationship has pulled the kid out, because it's so important to him. The boy was already a 'Make A Wish' child and had gone on his trip to Florida. And he is still alive today."

A Sense of Pride

Big Brothers often help Little Brothers not only feel better about themselves, but they help them feel better about their heritage. Derek Evans, a former Little Brother, grew up in the Cleveland area and was raised solely by his grandmother, who did the best she could. They were on food stamps and general assistance, but what hurt most was the teasing by Derek's schoolmates for not having any parents. His grandmother got him into the Youth Visions program in Cleveland, where he became a Little Brother at age ten. Derek had two different Big Brothers who lasted less than two years. He had all but given up until his caseworker, Robin Shavers, came over one day with his new Big Brother, Ozzie Newsome, then the star tight end for the Cleveland Browns.

"Ozzie came along when I was into selling drugs and material things, and he showed me there was another side, another way. He taught me that if you want something out of life, you have to work hard for it. I gained a sense of pride of being an African-American man. From the ordeal that I've had, I think being a Little saved my life." Derek has stayed involved with sports by coaching high school football. He is now the teacher. He is part of an alternative program for at-risk children in Yellow Springs High School, where he teaches kids about the importance of motivation and self-esteem.

Support at Critical Times

Fortunately for his Little Brother, Jack, Rick Steinkamp was there at the right time five years ago. Rick, who is now also a board member with Big Brothers Big Sisters of Southern Nevada, remembers helping Jack when Jack's mother had lung cancer. Jack's mother could not bring herself to tell her son, so she turned to Rick. She thought he would be able to help Jack through it, so Rick agreed to talk with Jack. He helped Jack through that time and also when Jack's mother died. Rick provided a stabilizing force during a very difficult time in Jack's life. Jack now lives with family in Kansas City, and he is doing well. He is completing ninth grade, gets straight A's and plays the viola.

Shawn

Shawn,[3] a Little Brother with Big Brothers, Big Sisters in Salt Lake City, Utah, was asked by his agency several years ago to write a letter about his experience with the program. The first letter was written when he was 10 years old and the second letter was written when he was 17.

s asked to tell you what it's like to live in a single-parent home with no money. Sometimes it's sad because I feel different from other kids. I have a Big Brother. He is not my real big brother. He is with the Big Brothers Association. Once I tried to tell my Big Brother about welfare. It was so embarrassing I was about to cry. I like Joe, not just because he takes me a fun place every week. I like Joe because he makes me feel special.

"Sometimes I pray that I won't be poor no more and sometimes I sit up at night and cry. But it didn't change anything. Crying just helps the hurt and the pain. It doesn't change anything. One day I asked my mom why the kids always tease me and she said because they don't understand. But I do understand about being on welfare and being poor and it can hurt."

Shawn, Age 10

At Age 17

"When I was 8 years old, the most influential and wonderful thing happened to me. An appointment was set. I was going to meet my new Big Brother. I was very scared because I had been on the waiting list for a long time. The thought of getting a Big Brother was exciting and terrifying at the same time.

"I didn't realize it at the time but things that were happening with my family were causing me a lot of stress and I started to react. We had to be on welfare while my mother was getting trained for work and not only was this a big embarrassment for me but all of a sudden we were poor. I became a holy terror in school and quite gifted at lying. I badly wanted a friend of my own.

"Seeing Joe was something I really looked forward to. I would get ready way ahead of time and then sit up on the roof so that I could see his car coming from far away. I couldn't wait to share with Joe all the things that happened over the past week. Joe would always sit there and listen to me. Before long I was telling him my deepest feelings. He always supported me and helped me find good ways to take control of my life. Over the past eight years, Joe has become my best friend. To say that he has put up with a lot from me is putting it very mildly. Somehow he hung in there. Joe has seen me through broken bones and broken hearts. He has cheered me at concerts and games. He has yelled at me for missing school then sat down with me to figure out why I was doing it and how I could change.

"He makes me learn for myself. He tells me 'think it out, you can do it' and I know that I can. He has helped me develop a confidence in myself that I can do and be anything. So look out world, and move over President Bush.

"Knowing Joe has meant that not only can I have friends, but I can be a friend. Not only can I receive, but I have a lot to give. Knowing Joe means that there will always be someone there to cheer me on to be the best that I can be—like Joe."

Shawn, Age 17

chapter

5

The Joy of Being a Big Brother

"Volunteering to be a Big Brother is in a sense one of the more

selfish things you can do because you wind up feeling great.

And the benefit is you're not just doing it for yourself, you have

someone to share it with."

Bill Sheil, on his relationship with his Little Brother, Jamie

≥⊙≤ ≥⊙≤ ≥⊙≤

Big Impact:
John Wells, 1996 National
Big Brother of the Year and LA[1]

Big Brothers of Greater Los Angeles, California

When John Wells, Executive Producer of the mega-hit NBC drama, ER, *decided to call Big Brothers of Greater Los Angeles seven years ago, he knew something was missing from his life. Even though he was putting in 60 to 80 hours a week, he still had Saturday afternoons free. While John felt very lucky about his accomplishments, which also include writing and producing the critically acclaimed ABC series,* China Beach, *he wanted to give something back to the community in a personal way, not just by writing checks.*

John wanted to give something back because he understands the value of one-to-one friendship. Back in college, one of John's professors, Fred Yeouns, took the time to give John some much needed attention. "I was pretty confused about what I wanted to do, and Fred took the time to look at me specifically and individually in what I was good at. He encouraged me in very specific ways that made a huge difference in my life because I wasn't seeing myself the way he did. When somebody sees you and shows up like that, you start to say to yourself, 'I must be worthwhile.'"

John got matched with LA, a nickname for Loren, when LA was seven years old. LA's father had died of AIDS when he was five, and later his uncle also died of AIDS. Most of the male figures in LA's life had slipped away, and his mother, Dorothea, began noticing behavior problems in LA, especially at school.

"Before John I had a really bad reputation. I was always starting trouble. But recently I've pulled it together, and I'm on the high honor roll at school. I'm on the student council, and I've won two awards for my artwork. I am a leader in my class."

Now a freshman in high school, LA's future goals include going to college and becoming an actor. He has already taken several acting classes.

John didn't realize how different the Big Brother experience would be from what he had imagined. "It's completely different than I thought it would be. I thought we'd be flying a kite with my hand on his shoulder. I was also afraid that I would fail or that he would be unmanageable—none of which has been the case. It's been much simpler than that."

It took John about a year to realize that just showing up was the most important thing. "I had in my own head an agenda of stuff to do and ways to make it all work, but I kept getting a little disappointed in that it didn't seem to make much difference to him if we were doing something that I thought was going to be special or not. After about a year, I realized that his attitude changed toward me, not because of anything special we did, but because he started to believe that I was going to keep showing up. It was just the consistency." After awhile John realized that on the occasional weeks when he didn't see LA, "I was amazed by how little I would actually accomplish on a Saturday afternoon."

John believes being a Big Brother helps create a much needed connection in society. "The collective responsibility of men to raising boys is increasingly missing in our culture, much to our great loss as a society. I think there's a lack of connection we all feel in the modern world and some of that has to do with the dissolution of the nuclear family and the fact that people's families are spread out all over the country. Becoming a Big Brother creates that extended family. It's very much like we're family. We get involved in birthdays and Christmas, and I'm a better person for it."

For LA, John is "like a part of my family. Even when he's away he always calls or sends postcards."

John advises other men not to look at being a Big Brother as any type of time burden. "I've found it easy and have made certain things a habit. Of all the things I do in my life, I get the most back for putting in the least amount of time. It's some of the most relaxing time I have, given the amount of time I work. It's like my planned recreation. It keeps me from being in the office on Saturdays, and it's not like anyone is going to say that I don't have my priorities straight."

The relationship has had a big impact on John. "It's changed me profoundly. In watching LA grow up, I feel like I've grown a lot and now have a different view of what it is to be a man. It has forced me to look at my responsibilities as an adult. I think it's hard for men to figure out what their identity is. As a result, the collective responsibility of men raising boys is increasingly missing from our culture. I see little things that LA has gotten from me, like gestures and speech patterns. In some ways, I feel like I've gotten a parenting class without having to be a parent. I've learned a lot about myself and setting boundaries. I've also learned the most important ingredient in a family—constant love and approval. And at the same time, I've learned that there have to be standards and requirements."

For Dorothea, the relationship has been a blessing. "What a wonderful relationship to be part of and watch," she says. "I can't imagine LA's life without John."

Certainly being the Little Brother of a Hollywood producer has its perks. LA has had a guest role on ER and has been to the Screen Actors' Guild Awards. But John and LA mostly do every-day activities, like going to the movies, running errands, and just talking. For John, being with LA is like "watching a tree grow. You don't notice the difference day to day, but over time you notice a substantial change."

John encourages other men to become Big Brothers because of how rewarding it is. "Having a car and a house and earning a living is all nice, but it's not all that fulfilling. You can't have a relationship with your car. There's something more to be had from life and (being a Big Brother) is one of those things that make life worth living."

LA and John have made a Big Impact on each other's lives.

$$\approx\!\textcircled{6}\!\approx \quad \approx\!\textcircled{6}\!\approx \quad \approx\!\textcircled{6}\!\approx$$

Hidden Benefits

Since childhood we have been reminded that, "It is better to give than to receive." Another popular adage tells us that "It is not what we give but what we share; for the gift without the giver is bare." Both ideas capture an important aspect of mentoring and volunteering as a Big Brother—that many joys and benefits result from sharing one's expertise, one's time, and oneself. This is one of the most overlooked aspects of becoming a Big Brother.

Many prospective Big Brothers think that the volunteer experience is a one-way exchange. They evaluate what they have to offer and give, without understanding what they might receive in return. Of course men do not become Big Brothers for personal gain as the primary focus. But if you have ever watched a Big and Little Brother together, you will notice that there are usually two people sharing, smiling, playing, and growing together. There are two people giving and receiving. Little Brothers have many gifts to share. By becoming a Big Brother, a man opens himself up to receiving gifts and experiences that will forever change his perspective on himself and the world around him.

While every Big Brother gets something unique from his match, there are many common threads that run throughout almost all Big/Little Brother relationships. Without hesitation, every Big Brother I interviewed believed they got as much, if not more, out of their relationship than their Little Brother did. What each Big Brother gets back depends a lot on their personal experiences—from their childhood to where they are in life today.

In this chapter, I will share with you what being a Big Brother means to some of the men who have volunteered. We will look at what they have learned, what they felt, how it has made a difference in their lives, and why they believe, as I do, that being a Big Brother is one of the most rewarding things a man will ever do.

Paying Back by Paying Forward

Many Big Brothers were fortunate in some way as they grew up. We were either raised in a supportive home with good values, or we lived in favorable circumstances. Many of us remember at least one adult who took a special interest in us—a relative, teacher, coach, or neighbor. That adult believed in us, paid attention to us, supported us when we needed it most and showed us that he or she cared.

Volunteering to be a Big Brother is a way for men to acknowledge just how fortunate they were, and, in many respects, still are. The best way to honor that is by doing what Emerson called "paying forward." We can pay back those who supported and guided us by sharing that with someone who will benefit from it.

Art Speelman, who was matched with Evan through Big Brothers Big Sisters of Beaver County, Pennsylvania, in 1980, believes, "It's not what you get out of life, it's what you put back in that makes you feel good. You can accumulate money and friends, but these things don't mean much if you don't put back in. If you give of yourself, you feel a whole lot better. In return, you get to watch a child change and grow before your eyes. And to know that he cares about you makes your life better."

For many men becoming a Big Brother is great way to give something back to the community. For some it is a chance to pay back and honor those who made a difference in their lives. Such was the case for Peter Sanders, a Big Brother with Catholic Big Brothers of New York City. Peter was raised in a single-parent household by his mother. When he was in high school, he was part of the Archbishop's Leadership Project for talented African-American teenagers. Father John Mehan, who led the program, also encouraged Peter to get involved with the Catholic Big Brothers program. Peter was matched with Damian back in November 1983. Damian would go on to graduate from Rice High School in Harlem and serve in the armed forces. Damian is now Lance Corporal Damian Lynch, USMC. For Peter, the experience has been very rewarding. "This was my opportunity to pay the Catholic church back for their support of me. I wanted to do something to give back. I knew I couldn't help save hundreds or thousands of kids, but I could help at least one."

Receiving the Greatest Gift

Being a Big Brother to Josh for the past five years has been extremely rewarding for Dan Winchester, because he was once a Little Brother himself. Like Josh, now 13 years old, Dan had experienced the adversity that divorce can have on a child. Having his Big Brother, Joe Glasser, helped Dan succeed through a "very emotional time." Dan believes that, "If I hadn't met Joe, I wouldn't have made it through high school." Not only did he make it through high school, he went on to Santa Monica College in California and is now a land-use planner with Ecology & Environment, Inc. in Tallahassee, Florida.

Because of his experience, Dan, now 31, felt compelled to reach out to another young person because, "I learned firsthand how a child's life can be enlightened if we could simply give what money will never buy—time." Over their five years together, Josh and Dan have shared many experiences, and Dan has always been there, through the ups and downs. Dan has seen Josh improve in his schoolwork and participate in numerous team sports. Recently, Josh called Dan "The greatest gift that I ever received."[2] To Dan, having Josh for a friend, "is the greatest gift in my life. My Big Brother always used to say 'Pass it on. Pass it on', and especially after what I went through, being able to give back is very rewarding."

Connecting with Boys

Whether they are parents or not, a lot of men feel disconnected from the boys in their community. Men do not understand their world, their lingo, their motivations, hopes, dreams, and fears. As a result men often form stereotypical images of today's boys. Becoming a Big Brother helps bring men back into direct contact with boys and makes them more caring and sensitive to a boy's future. Big Brothers also become advocates for their Little Brothers and more concerned about the issues and challenges that face the current generation of boys.

Sometimes that concern can make all the difference in the world. Dave Dubelle, a three-time Big Brother in Ohio, took the time to make an impact that will last a lifetime. Back in 1982, Dave's Little Brother, Todd, was having problems in school. Todd's parents divorced when he was eight years old. Todd would frequently get in trouble and defy authority. Between seventh and eighth grade, Todd received 20 F's. He was not doing well in his studies, he was disruptive in class, and he was spending lots of time in the detention center. Dave decided to talk with the vice principal and some of Todd's teachers. The general consensus was that Todd would not graduate to the ninth grade. In fact, his next scheduled classes were with students with learning disabilities. This would be the second time Todd was held back.

Dave believed that Todd just needed a chance to prove himself. He did not think Todd should be in special education classes. After much cajoling and effort on Dave's part, the teachers and administration met and voted on Todd's future destination. Dave guaranteed them Todd would succeed if given the chance. Dave met with Todd one day to ask him what would happen if he got the chance to go to high school instead of stay back. Todd decided that if he got the chance to go to high school, he would make the best of it.

It was decided by one vote, 4–3, to let Todd go into high school with the rest of his classmates on the condition that his grades improved in the last six weeks. Todd worked hard to do just that, and he went on the next year to make the honor role. Four years later, Todd graduated with his high school class. In the spring of 1996 Todd graduated from Kent State University with a degree in geology. He is hoping to work for the national parks department.

Todd gives a lot of credit to Dave. "Dave always stuck up for me when no one else did. Without Dave, I would never have gone to college, let alone probably finished high school. He showed me the value of hard work."

Dave considers himself "just an average person with no special skills who decided to care." While he may not consider himself a standout, Dave represents the type of support all boys need. Boys need someone in their corner, especially when the chips are down. And as a result, Dave has made an impact that forever changed Todd's life.

For other Big Brothers like Don Cummings, being a Big Brother provides an opportunity for those who have never had children. A Big Brother to six boys over the past 25 years with Big Brothers of Rhode Island, Don says, "I never married, and this afforded me the opportunity to reach out and interact with kids. All of my relationships have been great. It's wonderful to see the boys grow physically, spiritually, and morally. Whatever I have given to the program I have gotten back many times over."

Understanding the World of Boys

One Big Brother I talked with hit it right on the head when he said, "There are more distractions today than there ever were." As a result, most men have lost touch or connection with the boys in their neighborhoods. But for many men, the desire to have that connection is still there, and becoming a Big Brother is an opportunity to reach out to boys in a very personal, direct, and immediate way.

For Jimmy Watts, an African-American Big Brother in Jacksonville, Florida, being matched with Jammie has changed his awareness level toward kids. "It has really opened my eyes to teenage boys and what it's like to go through puberty today. You see that boys need direction from men."

For many Big Brothers, volunteering is the only chance they might have to get regular interaction with boys. That interaction often teaches Big Brothers a lot. Barry Gabel, a Big Brother with the Jewish Big Brothers Big Sisters Association in Cleveland, Ohio, believes, "More than anything, being a Big Brother has exposed me to situations I would never be in with a child. It has taught me to slow down, listen, and tune in to what is going on with children. It also has given me the chance to influence somebody and let them influence me. And now I have a friend for life."

Beyond the Neighborhood

Many of us view the world around us by what we see in the news. We take these bits and pieces and collectively judge what another town or area must be like. By doing so, we often miss getting a real sense of what goes on in different communities.

Jon Friedland, a former Little Brother who is now a Big Brother with Big Brothers Big Sisters of Greater Miami, Florida, is happy to have the opportunity to see other areas. "The Big Brothers Big Sisters program has helped me break down some barriers. I get to visit an area of town that I didn't visit and really see firsthand what goes on."

When Big Brothers visit other areas of their communities, they come away with a deeper understanding and appreciation of various neighborhoods. Many Big Brothers, after spending time in neighboring communities, learn that these communities offer much more than is shown on television. They also develop a more compassionate perspective and work more effectively with their Little Brothers.

Mike Solomon, a Big Brother in Hereford, Texas, with Big Brothers Big Sisters of Hereford, believes both he and his family have benefited from his match with Chad, who is now 22. "Chad has been good for me, too. It gives you a reward in life that you would never have otherwise. It was also good for my two children. They thought everyone was raised the same and lived the same life, and this gave them an opportunity to see how other children lived."

New Perspectives on Parenting

While many Big Brothers have children themselves, volunteering often provides men with the opportunity to reflect on their own parenting skills.

For Bob Chiappinelli, a Big Brother with two children of his own, volunteering provided a new perspective. "With my own kids I'm always setting limits and making judgment calls, braking their headlong rush to become adults at the ages of 10 and 12. It's different with a Little Brother. You pop into the life of a boy who is living without a father in his home, share good moments and pop out again. You escape the daily discipline of parenting. You relax and enjoy. You realize that, just like in parenting, you have to be more than an authority figure. Compared to being an overly concerned parent, being a Big Brother is often a breath of fresh air."

Volunteering gives Big Brothers the opportunity to see and appreciate the role that parents play in a boy's life, especially for those who are not parents yet. For Mike Propp, a Big Brother in Manhattan, Kansas, "Being with Charles taught me a lot about being a father without him knowing it. I learned how important it was to listen and develop trust. I saw how important it was to give Charles the feeling that there was always somebody he could talk to." Even though Charles is 19, he still relies on Mike for occasional fatherly advice. Mike himself now has two children—a stepdaughter and a six year-old son.

Being a Big Brother to Greg gave Dan Shemer, a Big Brother in Maryland, a taste of what parenting might be like. To him, it was "like a dry run. I got to watch a brain grow. I think I'm a better parent now because of Greg." Dan now has a 15-year-old daughter, but he is equally proud of Greg, who now works as a computer consultant. They have known each other more than 18 years.

A Sense of Accomplishment

Most of us work hard every day at our jobs, but we often feel a lack of accomplishment or feeling of satisfaction that we have truly made a difference somewhere, somehow, about something that really matters. For many men, being a Big Brother helps fill that void, that need to make an impact on the world.

A Big Brother may not know for many years the full impact that he has made on a Little Brother's life. But whether you have been matched for a few months or many years, there are often signs that give you a sense that you have made a difference.

Nate Horowitz, a Big Brother with the Jewish Big Brothers Big Sisters Association of Boston since 1978, remembers a time he noticed a difference in his first Little Brother. After the boy's parents divorced, he went from one school to another. He tried to burn down one of his schools. Neither parent wanted the boy. Around Chanukah time one year, Nate came over and gave the boy a calculator. The boy was living with seven other children in a one-room apartment and was having a difficult time. He went off in the corner to check out the calculator. A little while later, Nate noticed something peculiar—the boy was not only playing the math game, but he was sharing the toy with his sister and her friends. Nate was amazed because this was "categorically impossible." The boy was not good in math, would never give up a toy, and would never get over the fact that his sister had friends and he did not. Despite all that he was supposed to be, here he was doing the exact opposite. Nate felt, "It was very satisfying to watch." Nate believes that children can begin to succeed when they have a consistent relationship with an adult. Nate believes children need to be turned toward the light to grow—just as plants flourish in sunshine.

Jerry Cleveland, a Big Brother to Anthony for over ten years, feels a strong sense of accomplishment, because he was once a single parent himself. "You get a sense of satisfaction when you see somebody that you take an interest in learn to do things, and in some cases, even do them better than you as a teacher. There's a sense of pride knowing that you influenced someone or put that spark in them, so that they can apply their energy in a way that helps someone else."

Some Little Brothers do not express gratitude to their Big Brothers for many, many years, while other Little Brothers, for numerous reasons, many never *outwardly* express their gratitude. When they do, it often comes as a wonderful surprise. Chuck Reisdorf, a Big Brother to Keith, will never forget what Keith said to him after nine years of being matched. "When Keith told me I was the biggest influence in his life and that he looked up to me, it was incredible. There is an extraordinary feeling of accomplishment about something that matters, the development of a child."

Proud Moments

Big Brothers take great pride in spending time with and sharing in the accomplishments of their Little Brothers. Mike Radakovich, a 43-year-old Big Brother in Stuarts Draft, Virginia, with Big Brothers Big Sisters of the Central Blue Ridge, developed what he called "the proud father" syndrome with his Little Brother Bill over the past ten years. "I began relating to how people feel about their children's accomplishments. I remember how proud I was when Bill made the track team in high school and when he got into college."

Some Big Brothers experience a feeling of pride when they take part in their Little Brothers' significant events. Eric Silver, a Big Brother with the Jewish Big Brothers Big Sisters Association in Cleveland, Ohio, recalled a time last year with his Little Brother, Eddie, with whom he has been matched since 1989. "Recently, I was given the honor of sharing the Bima with Eddie on his Bar Mitzvah. It was an unexpected pleasure to be part of one of the most important events in Eddie's life to date. He sang his portion with confidence and an adult-like air that confirmed the fact that he was now a man. While Eddie sang, I reflect-ed on the changes I witnessed in him over six years and realized how proud I am to be his Big Brother and his friend."[3]

Eric strongly believes that he has benefited from his relationship with Eddie. "It is one of the few things in life that is all good. There is no cost to my investment in our relationship. It's all positive return for me. Early on it built my confidence to develop a relationship with him. And now knowing that I have had some impact on his life makes me feel great."

Big Brothers often experience little moments that make them feel great. Richard Hlavsa remembered how his Little Brother, Jonathan, nine years old at the time, reacted when he found out Richard's actu-al age. "We were at a Big Brothers Big Sisters Halloween outing. Jonathan thought I was about 20 until he found out I was 64 and older than his grandmother. When he heard that he said to me, 'When you die, I will go to your funeral. In fact, I'll direct it.' And that made me feel great, to know he wants to take charge when I'm gone."

Tables Turned

Big Brothers go through difficult and challenging times in life just as their Little Brothers do. It is important for a Little Brother to see the ups and downs of a Big Brother's life, and how a Big Brother handles himself. But just as Big Brothers are often there to help their Littles in difficult times, a Little Brother can make a big impact on a Big Brother's life.

Bruce Bridges, a Big Brother in Marlborough, Massachusetts, with Big Brothers Big Sisters of Middlesex County, learned what an impact a Little Brother could make soon after he was matched. Just eight weeks after he met his Little Brother, Johnny, Bruce's wife Julie died in an accident. Johnny had met Julie a few times, and Bruce thought that her death would be too overwhelming for him, given that Johnny had already lost his father and grandfather. When Bruce told Johnny about it a week later, it was Bruce who was overwhelmed by Johnny's reac-tion. Johnny, just 11 years old at the time, told him, "Bruce, I know how you feel. I know how you hurt, but remember, Julie is in heaven now."

Bruce was surprised to see their roles reversed. "I got into the pro-gram to make a difference in a little guy's life, and here he was making a difference in mine. He was more of a man than I had given him credit for. He understood more than I had realized he would."

New Skills and Experiences

Big Brothers often learn a lot of interpersonal skills. They learn how to work effectively with boys and discover what is really important to boys. Paul Beck, a Big Brother in Topeka, Kansas, says "I learned a lot about myself and others. It put me in situations that I had never dealt with before. Some were difficult situations, but I learned tools on how to deal with them. As a result, it has helped me grow as much as it has Michael."

Dan Reida, a Big Brother through Big Brothers Big Sisters of Cape Cod and the Islands, learned a lot of life skills through his nearly 20-year relationship with John Frasier. "I learned about how important consistency was in his life. I learned what just concentrating on John for three or four hours could do. If you spend that much time concentrating on that person, you are going to have a better relationship."[4]

Jim Webb and Joey Wauters, the couples match from Alaska we met in the last chapter, fondly recall the impact that their Little Brother Shajan Kay, had on them. "He got us into things we would have never done, like skiing. We went to see his plays in school and at summer art camp. As adults without children, we would never have gone to anything like that." Although Shajan is now attending college in Michigan, Jim and Joey still go to see high school plays just to watch the children's enthusiasm. Jim is also considering pursuing a teaching degree, which he would not have been interested in were it not for the time he spent with Shajan.

A Wish Fulfilled

The relationship with a Little is the closest experience to having a real son that some men will ever have. This was part of Art Speelman's motivation to become a Big Brother. "I realized I missed a lot by not having a son," Art said. "I missed not going out in the woods, walking in the woods, doing the things that my dad and I did." Through their friendship of more than 16 years, Art and Evan have enjoyed many activities in the great outdoors. Art has also been at many of Evan's special moments, including his high school and college graduations. And Evan has been there when Art needed him, like when Art had a heart attack and had bypass surgery. Although Art is now 66 and Evan 28, there will always be a special bond between them. Art believes in his heart that "If we'd had a son, we would have liked him to be like Evan."

Sometimes a match fulfills the wish for other types of relationships. I myself am an only child, and so my relationship with Tony gives me a chance to get a feel for what it is like to have a brother. Growing up I remember what it was like to not have anyone at home to play with or share things with, or even just to listen. By sharing my time with Tony I get to do some of the things I would have wanted to do if I had had a brother.

A Better Appreciation of Life

Being a Big Brother is one of the most humbling experiences you can have. As Chuck Crockett expressed about his match, "It keeps my level of humility. You understand that things aren't always so easy. It has allowed me to focus on what is really important in life. I see how Gabe treats life and doesn't complain about it. Comparatively I see that I have it very easy."

Tim Roth, who has been matched with Jason since 1993 through Big Brothers Big Sisters of the Ozarks, in Springfield, Missouri, believes that, "Being a Big Brother makes me feel good about myself. It has helped me grow a lot because I realize what a lot of my gifts are, especially my parents and upbringing. I have a better appreciation of life, because I can see that life is tough for some kids even though it's not their fault. It's opened my eyes to another world. It reminds me to be thankful for what I have."

For other Big Brothers, it is simply an awareness of the value that a quality one-to-one relationship can bring. Jerome Scriptunas, a two-time Big Brother who currently serves as president of the board of Big Brothers Big Sisters of Monmouth County, New Jersey, believes he has learned the "extraordinary importance of ordinary experiences." Jerome feels, "To see how a relationship can evolve over time simply through doing ordinary, everyday things, is a wonderful gift."

The Most Rewarding Thing I Have Ever Done

Mitch McMurray, a former Little Brother and current Big Brother with Big Brothers Big Sisters of Greater Miami, Florida, summed it up best when he told me, "It's a tremendously fulfilling and satisfying way to give back to the community. It helps every man address that fear of commitment to be able to stick to something. It's a very valuable, maturing experience whether you are a young adult, in your 30s or

40s or whatever. It gives you the opportunity to make a direct impact on someone's life outside of your family. It is a big commitment, but once you start, it takes on a life of its own. It just becomes a part of your life, part of the routine. If there is any aspect of my life that I have received respect from, it is from being a Big Brother."

Big Brothers have an opportunity to connect with kids, learn new skills, and share in new experiences. They derive a great sense of pride and accomplishment, and a better appreciation for life. It is such a powerful experience that it is not unusual to hear comments like Todd Hebert's who told me, "It's easily the most rewarding thing I've ever done."

chapter

6

Spending Time with a Little Brother

"Some of the best moments are driving home together and listening to him talk. (Places like) Disneyland are nice and all, but you don't have to be there to have a special moment. I'm just a big kid anyway, and being a Big Brother is a great opportunity to do activities that I normally might not do."

Eric Asch, a Big Brother in Scottsdale, Arizona

=⊚⟨= =⊚⟨= =⊚⟨=

Big Impact:
Greg and Chase

Big Brothers Big Sisters
of Polk County, Lakeland, Florida

*You never know what will happen when you expose a child
to something new. That is what Big Brother Greg Crowe discovered from his match with Little Brother Chase. Greg knew
12-year-old Chase had an interest in music when they were
matched in 1990 with Big Brothers Big Sisters of Polk County in
Lakeland, Florida. Greg and Chase spent a lot of time at record
stores and record shows. At the time, Chase was a fan of the rock
group, Heart.*

*But things would change forever when Greg and his wife
Shelly took Chase to the symphony in Lakeland, Florida.
According to Greg, "Chase was really struck by the whole symphony experience." After that, Chase started getting more serious
about music. He started taking piano lessons, and he often prac-
ticed on Shelly's piano. Greg believed that Chase, "had a real
knack for it, he seemed very gifted."*

*Before long, Greg was writing and working on his own
music. He auditioned for the local arts school, the Harrison
School for the Performing Arts, and was accepted. From the time
Chase first expressed an interest in music, his mother was very
supportive and encouraging. She even bought him a secondhand piano.*

*This outcome was somewhat of a surprise to Greg. When they
were first matched, Greg thought Chase did not seem like he was
concerned about getting through high school. His grades were
not very good and he would have to go to school on Saturdays
because he often acted out in class. He was not focused and did
not apply himself.*

*But Greg decided not to come down hard on him or disci-
pline him. He told Chase what he thought and shared how he felt.
As a result of Greg's supportive approach, Chase more easily
opened up and discussed his feelings.*

Today Chase is still pursuing his love for music and the piano while attending Florida Southern College on two different music scholarships. Although Greg now lives in Tennessee, he and Shelly occasionally travel to see Chase's recitals.

Greg will be the first to tell you that others deserve the credit for Chase's success. "We just did average things together. I don't feel like I did a lot. I just exposed him to things and he took it from there. His mother and his teachers were so supportive." Greg believes the experience for him "has been really fulfilling. It's helped me to round myself out in the community by making a positive contribution. Once I got involved, I really realized what I was missing just working all the time, evenings and weekends. I wasn't making any effort to do anything from a community standpoint. But once I got involved, I realized how much better I felt making a positive contribution. And I like the program because of the one-on-one contact."

Greg wants people to know that being a Big Brother is easier than they might think. "People think they have to entertain the Little all the time, but it's really not like that. There were a lot of times where we just had Greg over to eat, like making a pizza together, and he really enjoyed those times. Sure we did stuff like go to the symphony, but we played a lot of board games and watched movies together, too."

By exposing Chase to the magic of the symphony, but more importantly, by spending quality time together, Greg helped Chase develop the confidence to explore a field for which he truly has a passion. While Greg does not think he deserves a lot of credit, his presence in Chase's life has made a Big Impact.

≧ⓞ≦ ≧ⓞ≦ ≧ⓞ≦

Shared Interests

What do Big Brothers do every week with their Little Brothers? This question is often an intimidating one to both prospective and new Big Brothers. Fortunately, a Big Brother has all the skills and resources necessary to have many successful and mutually rewarding experiences. Through the Big Brothers Big Sisters matching process, a Big Brother will be matched with a boy who shares some similar interests. Those interests are a great starting point to build on, but Big Brothers are certainly not limited to just those activities.

The most important aspect of spending time with a Little Brother is attitude. There are two things that a Big Brother should always keep in mind. First, it is not a Big Brother's role to save the world every week, and second, a Big Brother is a friend and not an entertainer. Taking that weight off of a Big Brother's shoulders allows him to focus on the simple and easy things he can do to create a fun, fulfilling relationship.

This chapter is not just about the types of activities that Big and Little Brothers do. It is about how these activities play a role in the development of a young boy. Through the eyes of many Big Brothers, you will learn what is really important about the way time should be spent with a Little Brother. What a Big Brother will find is that, more often than not, what stands out for a Little Brother is not so much *what* they do together, but the simple fact that they are doing something *together.*

Time Is Everything

It is essential to remember that money cannot buy a Little Brother's friendship. Spending a lot of money will only establish a pattern that has him associate each get together with spending money. While a Little Brother may even encourage his Big Brother to do or buy things that cost a lot of money, a Big Brother should emphasize to his Little Brother that he is there as a friend. The best guideline, according to Big Brothers Big Sisters of Santa Fe, New Mexico, is to "Look at your (Big Brother Big Sister) relationship as two friends involved in planning activities; the two friends should determine together how they can afford it according to their own individual means."

Meredith Lopes, grandmother of Little Brother Errol through Big Brothers of Rhode Island, recalls the importance of the time Errol spent with Big Brother Ken Shapiro. "It wasn't about money or what they did, it was the quality time that they spent together. What was important was not spending money but that Errol knew that this was a special person just for him; that somebody cared enough about him to spend some time. Knowing that helped his self-confidence."

Spending quality time with a Little Brother is the most important thing a Big Brother can do.

Money's Not the Object

All Big Brothers are encouraged to plan activities and outings that cost little or no money. As Pat Myers, director of Big Brothers Big Sisters of Madison County, Indiana, says, "Adult volunteers don't necessarily have to do activities that cost a lot of money. We stress that the time is more important than spending money on the child. There are many free or inexpensive activities. We want Little Brothers to understand and appreciate that friendship is not based on money and what is going to be bought for them."[1]

Plan Activities Together

It is a good practice to plan activities jointly with a Little Brother. Doing so gives him a feeling of responsibility and choice. Activities should be fun and provide learning experiences. A Little Brother may need time to think over suggested activities, and a Big Brother should be patient as his Little Brother considers activities. A Little Brother may want to try something new but may not be comfortable doing so. A Big Brother can offer sympathy and understanding to help encourage his Little Brother to participate. A Big Brother can offer to teach his Little Brother to do new things, but he should not push him.

Have Fun

One element that Big Brothers should always remember is the importance of simply having fun when they are with their Little Brothers. Big Brother Bill Sheil reminds us that, "We all like to have fun, but how often do we actually say 'I am going to have fun today'?" A Big Brother should welcome the opportunity to do fun things, and in the process he may lose any inhibitions he might have had.

My Little Brother Tony encourages me to do things I usually only did as a child—like riding a roller coaster, going on water slides, fishing, model building, camping, snowman building, sundae eating, pumpkin carving—and the list goes on and on. I feed off of the energy and excitement that Tony has doing these activities.

Big Brothers should take advantage of the enthusiasm their Little Brothers have toward their favorite activities. By doing so, a Big Brother shares the joys of these activities and becomes an active participant.

Little Things Make a Big Impact

Sometimes "less is more." Often different experiences make an impression that is far more lasting than one would ever think possible. I was amazed at how many former Little Brothers recounted stories that their Big Brothers had forgotten. The stories were not about extravagant trips, but about talks during car rides or dinners at a Big Brother's house. Dan Beard, a Big Brother in Palm Bay, Florida, admits that with Jessie, his current Little Brother, "We do most of our talking during drives in the car."

Dan Wright, a Big Brother to Philip for more than four years through Big Brothers Big Sisters of Charlotte County, Florida, points out, "With Philip, we don't always have to do special things. Sometimes he'll just come over to my place and we'll sit around and rent movies or do yardwork or play on the computer together." Dan thinks that simply spending time with Philip, now ten years old, has helped him come out of his shell.

Big Brothers often make the mistake of doing too much or trying too hard. It was very early in their relationship when Eddie Friend, who has been Lee Willingham's Big Brother for more than 17 years, learned this important lesson. "I remember taking him to a University of Alabama football game our first time out. The second time we went to the zoo, and I spent all this time learning about snakes because he said they were his favorite. And then the third outing I just brought him along with me to the laundromat. He told me, 'This is the best thing we've done!' He told me he had a great time just talking. I realized then that I needed to stop performing." Instead, Eddie and Lee occasionally perform together. The two have spoken throughout Birmingham on behalf of Big Brothers Big Sisters of Greater Birmingham. Lee, now 26 years old, is working for a regional distributor of industrial equipment.

Get Involved in Agency Group Activities

Many agencies have group activities for Big and Little Brothers. Not only is this a great opportunity to do something fun, but it is also a chance to meet other matches and make new friends, both for the Big and Little Brothers.

Big Brothers Big Sisters of Santa Fe, New Mexico, has several Bigs who are retirees. One of the agency's most successful projects is their

Fly Fishing Youth Mentoring Project,[2] now in its fifth year. In collaboration with the Sangre de Cristo Fly Fishing Club, kids learn the fine art of fly fishing. Members teach the children to tie flies, to respect nature through stream ecology and entomology lessons, and to properly cast their fly rods. Children and their mentors go on at least three major fishing trips to New Mexico lakes and streams using the flies they have tied.

The goal of the project is to provide children with high expectations for success through a high ratio of mentors to children. The experience also provides all children with support and caring through adult and peer mentors. It helps teach life skills such as responsibility, decision-making, commitment, communication, and interaction. The program also promotes social skills, such as cooperation, conflict resolution, relationship building, and values clarification, to increase bonds with adults and peers.

Some agencies also have Big Brother Councils, which are informal groups of Big Brothers that meet or share activities on a regular basis. Big Brothers of the National Capitol Area in Maryland has several councils, one of which, the Prince George's County Big Brother Council, was founded and is run by Big Brother Nicholas Panebianco. The council's mission is to advance, enhance, and support the efforts of Big and Little Brother matches. The most popular event that the council plans is its annual camping trip with Little Brothers. The weekend always turns out to be a great success, both for the Big and Little Brothers. Nick says, "It's tiring, but it is great to watch the kids interact and have fun, and the guys get to hang out and talk, too." If a local Big Brothers Big Sisters agency has a Big Brother Council, Big Brothers are advised to get in touch with them directly. If such a council does not exist, a volunteer should consider starting some informal group with other Bigs to plan get-togethers or activities.

Big Brothers should take advantage of the activities that each agency offers. Many agencies receive discount tickets to local events and attractions. Also, most agencies have at least two regular group get-togethers, typically an outing in the summer and a holiday party in the winter.

Know the Community

Whether a Big Brother lives in the same town or 50 miles away from his Little Brother, they likely have had very different experiences within their own communities. Big Brothers should take the time to learn about their Little Brother's community or neighborhood. A Big Brother can let his Little Brother show him around and be the tour guide. No matter where he lives, he probably has his own favorite places. When a Little Brother shares his world, a Big Brother can discover the places and people that matter to his Little Brother.

Bryan Ross, a 13-year-old Little Brother in Woodridge, Illinois, has introduced his Big Brother, Jamie Hensley, to several places in his neighborhood. Bryan told Jamie about his barber, and now the two have their hair cut together every four or five weeks. Afterward they go out to Bryan's favorite place for hot dogs and ice cream.[3]

A Big Brother should take the time to become familiar with his Little Brother's life. It gives a Little Brother a sense of pride when he shows his Big Brother "his world." It will also give him a chance to open up to his Big Brother in a way that makes him feel comfortable.

The Big's World

It is just as important that a Little Brother learn what his Big Brother's life is like. A Big Brother should show his Little Brother where he works and talk about what he does for a living. If possible a Big Brother should arrange for a Little Brother to visit him at work, perhaps during a school vacation.

When a Little Brother is ready a Big Brother should welcome his Little Brother into his home and show him around his neighborhood. A Big Brother can show his Little Brother the things that matter to him—favorite places to go, eat, and visit. Jamie Hensley introduced his Little Brother Bryan to one of his big joys, golf, and they often play together after Jamie gets off of work.

Sharing a Big Brother's life experiences helps a Little Brother feel comfortable with his Big Brother. Paul Beck has known his Little Brother Michael for 12 years. Throughout their time together, Paul has introduced Michael to many aspects of his life. He has taken him to his job where he works for the state as a computer programmer and trainer. Paul took the time to expose Michael to the world of computers. Michael has spent time with Paul's mother, brother, and sister-in-law. Paul also introduced his Little Brother to one of his favorite interests, martial arts, which helped teach Michael self-discipline and focus.

While it is important for a Big Brother to show a Little Brother the things that make him happy, it is also good to show what makes him sad. Lyle Green remembers the time that he and his brother Eric, both Little Brothers to Neil Young, went to visit each other's father's graves. "Neil's father passed away when he was younger, so he understood what it was like. Visiting our fathers' graves was a great idea. We saw that he could relate to us, and that meant a lot."

Taking the time to show a Little Brother different aspects of a Big Brother's life helps him learn more about his Big Brother and the world beyond his own neighborhood.

New People and New Places

A Big Brother can help a Little Brother develop social skills by introducing him to new people, such as friends, business associates, and family. Exposing a Little Brother to new people gives him an opportunity to see how other people live, work, and play. Exposure to new people helps a Little Brother develop a greater sense of what he likes and does not like.

Peter Becker, a Big Brother through Big Brothers Big Sisters of Middlesex County, Massachusetts, used to always bring his Little Brother, Hashim, to barbecues, outings, and Holy Cross football games with his family. Peter believed it was important to include him in these types of settings. "I think it helped give Hashim a more positive view of adults and helped him deal with adults better. It also got him to talk about experiences that he would probably never normally talk to other adults about." Spending time with Peter's family became such a regular occurrence for Hashim that he told one of his friends who came to a Holy Cross game with him, "Be prepared to do a lot of talking and a lot of handshaking." This type of interaction with adults has a lasting impact. Hashim was very shy when he first met Peter, but by the fall of 1993, Hashim and Peter were speaking publicly together at a United Way annual meeting to recognize the length of their match.

A Big Brother should introduce his Little Brother to people in different fields and professions. This simple exposure can have a tremendous impact on Little Brothers who can learn firsthand about careers and how individuals reached their positions. As a result, Little Brothers often learn that success can be achieved through hard work and dedication.

Include a Little Brother in Activities

Sometimes, no matter what, it is difficult to come up with something to do with a Little Brother. One of the easiest things a Big Brother can always do is include his Little in things that he does on a regular basis, like going to the gym, housework, or errands. Again, what stands out for a Little Brother is not always the specific activity, but the fact that time is being spent together. Most Bigs are amazed when they tell their Little Brothers, "I was just going to do some errands or stuff around the house today, do you want to come?" and they get back an immediate and enthusiastic, "Yes! Yes!"

Over the 27 years that C. J. Bundy has known his Big Brother, Senator Daniel Coats of Indiana, spending time with Dan's family was always a great experience. "Dan's family accepted me right away, and I was very excited about it. Coming from a dysfunctional family, I never saw a lot of love articulated or demonstrated, but Dan's family just showed it to each other. I recognized the difference, and I enjoyed it. Marsha, Dan's wife, was the first female adult who was just nice to me and loving, and not a disciplinarian. Watching his family interact made me want to interact that way with my family. I really enjoyed spending time with Dan's family. They taught me what family is all about. They didn't have to 'show' me. They were just themselves."

Big Brothers who include their Little Brothers in activities help encourage the Little Brothers to try new things and build self-confidence. Jerry Cleveland, a Big Brother in Verona, Virginia, with Big Brothers Big Sisters of the Central Blue Ridge, remembers how easy it was to integrate his Little Brother Anthony into his life. "I didn't stop or change what I was doing. I just included him, whether it was work or play. He was a tremendous help to me on my farm. I taught him how to drive the tractor and do other things around the farm. But we also did fun things like fish and hunt." As a result of these experiences, Anthony has become very accomplished and coordinated in operating machinery and driving vehicles. Jerry believes these things helped Anthony, now 21 and working for a large bakery, develop an increased sense of self-confidence. That self-confidence led Anthony to join the air force after high school. In addition to his current job, Anthony also serves as a volunteer fireman.

Try Something New Together

There are lots of places that both a Big and Little Brother have probably never visited or explored. Learning or trying something new together is not only a great bonding activity, it is also exciting because

Author Rich Greif and Little Brother Tony Merrill at Tony's 8th grade graduation, June 1996.

Big Brother Eric Asch with Little Brother Brent of Valley Big Brothers Big Sisters in Phoenix, Arizona.

Big Brother Jimmy Watts of Big Brothers Big Sisters of Greater Jacksonville, Florida, receiving the 1995 Big Brother of the Year award along with his Little Brother, Jammie.

Little Brother Jason with Big Brother Tim Roth of Big Brothers Big Sisters of the Ozarks in Springfield, Missouri, back in 1993. Tim and Jason are pictured after completing their first race together. At age 9, Jason received first place in the 13 and under age group. It was his first trophy, and he proudly displays it to this day.

Big Brother Rob Frier and his Little Brother Yonah of the Jewish Big Brothers Big Sisters League of Baltimore enjoying a festival on the Washington, DC mall.

Passing It On. Big Brother Matt Bradley (left) is pictured with his Little Brother Gerry Murphy (far right). Gerry went on to be a Big Brother to Jason (center). All three are pictured at Gastons Resort on the White River in Arkansas. Matt now lives in Little Rock, while Gerry and Jason are from Topeka, Kansas. All were matched through Big Brothers Big Sisters of Topeka.

Little Brother Josh of the Big Brothers Association of Greater Boston enjoying a sunny day in Boston this past summer.

Little Brother John, age 13, with his Big Brother Bruce Bridges, 54, at a recent Halloween party with Big Brothers Big Sisters of South Middlesex, Massachusetts.

National Spokesman and National Board Member Lynn Swann speaks at the 1996 Big Brothers Big Sisters of America National Conference in Washington, DC.

Senator Daniel Coats of Indiana, himself a Big Brother, speaks at the 1996 Big Brothers Big Sisters of America Conference in Washington, DC. He is also a member of the National Board of Directors at Big Brothers Big Sisters of America.

*Big Brother (and for-
mer Little Brother)
Dan Winchester with
Little Brother Josh.
Dan and Josh have
been matched
through Big Brothers
Big Sisters of the Big
Bend in Tallahassee,
Florida, since 1992.*

*Little Brother Chad and
Big Brother Mike Solomon
have been matched
through Big Brothers Big
Sisters of Hereford, Texas,
since 1987.*

Little Brothers learn the fine art of fly fishing as part of Big Brothers Big Sisters of Santa Fe, New Mexico's Fly Fishing Youth Mentoring Project, in collaboration with the Sangre de Cristo Fly Fishing Club.

Six-time Big Brother Bob Chiappinelli of Big Brothers of Rhode Island is pictured with his current Little Brother, A.J., at Disney World in 1994. As part of its anniversary celebration, Disney World flew in Big and Little Brother representatives from all over the United States.

Big Brothers, Big Celtics. Boston Celtic Pervis Ellison is pictured teaching a Little Brother basketball skills during an annual skills clinic that the Celtics put on for the Big Brothers Association of Greater Boston.

© *Chris Advama*

Big Brother Thomas Shadrick with Little brother Jeremy, of Big Brothers Big Sisters of South Hampton Roads, Virginia.

Rich and Tony back in 1991 at the New England Aquarium.

Big Brother and WEWS Newscaster Bill Sheil with his Little Brother, Jamie, matched through Youth Visions in Cleveland, Ohio, for over six years.

Big Brother Chuck Crockett is the Jolly Green Giant and his Little Brother Gabe is Sprout, pictured with Big Brother Mike Daigle and his Little Brother Jason at the 1989 Big Brothers Big Sisters of South Middlesex Halloween party. Gabe and Chuck have been matched since 1989.

Chuck with Gabe at Gabe's high school graduation in 1996. Gabe is now in Marine camp in Parris Island.

Big Brother Louis Lucarelli with Little Brother Mike, who have been matched through Youth Visions in Cleveland since 1986.

Big Brother Jeff Lambrecht taking a scuba diving class with 14 year old Little Brother Jack, who have been matched through Big Brothers Big Sisters of Metropolitan Detroit since 1994.

Big Brother Peter Sanders (left) with Little Brother Lance Corporal Damian Lynch, USMC, who have been matched through Catholic Big Brothers in New York City since 1983. They are the longest match in the agency's 85 year history.

Big Couple, Big Family, Big Impact. Big Brother and Big Sister couples match Betty and George Monroe pictured at a pool party in 1988 with Little Brother Brett (far right), along with Brett's brother (center) and the Monroes' granddaughter and friend. The Monroes now live in Michigan. They were matched with Brett for 9 years through Big Brothers Big Sisters of Charlotte County, Florida.

Big Brother Rick Steinkamp and Little Brother Jack were matched in 1991 through Big Brothers Big Sisters of Southern Nevada. Although Jack has since moved, the Big / Little stay in contact. Rick is now a member of the Board of Directors at his agency.

John Wells, 1996 National Big Brother of the Year and Executive Producer of the television show ER, with Little Brother, LA, matched through Big Brothers of Greater Los Angeles since 1991.

© *Long Photography, Inc.*

Big Brother Kenny Gordon and Little Brother Phillip Henry on one of their first outings in 1983. They have been friends for over 14 years through Chattanooga Big Brothers Big Sisters in Tennessee. Kenny is currently matched to his third Little Brother, Ryan. Phillip is attending the University of Georgia.

Throughout their friendship, Kenny Gordon has exposed Phillip to many places. Here Phillip is attending a black-tie affair with Kenny in New York City.

Big Brother Don Cummings, a Big Brother for over 25 years with Big Brothers of Rhode Island, is pictured here several years ago with Little Brothers Dane, Phanna, and Phanny Prep.

Devin Rowling, former Little Brother and owner of the Cosi Cucina Italian Grill in Des Moines, Iowa, stands next to a portrait of a Big and Little Brother done by local artist Doug Paul to promote Big Brothers Big Sisters of Greater Des Moines.

© Doug Paul

Big Brother Paul Oberg, with Big Brothers of Rhode Island, who was matched to Little Brother Nate until Nate's passing in 1992.

Little Brother Nate trying out golf while on a trip to Florida with Big Brother Paul Oberg and wife Betsey.

Little Brother Nate is pictured in front as best man at Big Brother Paul Oberg's wedding to Betsey in 1982.

both the Big and Little Brother share in the new experience.

Little Brothers often encourage Big Brothers to lose their inhibitions and try something new. Jeff Venable remembers such a time with his Little, Joseph. "I remember riding bikes along the river with a three-foot walking path and some rough areas. We're riding on the path where there is some brush and, as we glance over there, we see three or four heads bop up on this really narrow path on the bank as it descends toward the river. Joseph looks at me with big, wide eyes and I say, 'No, we shouldn't do that.' Needless to say, five minutes later I'm following him down this path, and I realize we're having a blast. I was too scared to go first, but he had no problem. We spent about three or four hours tearing up and down this path. I'm learning how to play from this kid. As we finished, I looked at him and said, 'I'm so glad we didn't listen to me, because we would have missed out on all this fun.'"

Some Big and Little Brothers start their own ventures together. Big Brother Dave Watson and Little Brother Princewill Daniells of Big Brothers Big Sisters of Middlesex County, Massachusetts, are utilizing their interest in bubble gum to start a bubble gum business. They had such a great time making homemade bubble gum that they are now calling themselves the "Bubblicious Buddies."[4]

No matter how old a Little Brother is, there will be many activities he has never tried or even knew existed. A Big Brother should take the time to introduce his Little Brother to as many new experiences as possible. Keep in mind that just like anyone trying something new, a Little Brother may not end up liking the activity. A Big Brother needs to let his Little Brother know that it is okay to say he does not like something and that his honesty will be respected.

Coming up with "new" activities is not as difficult as one might think. Paul Dascoli introduced his Little Brother Brian to pumpkin carving and Easter egg coloring. Even though Brian was 11 at the time, he had never experienced these things. Jim Formato took his Little Brother to the beach for the first time.

Sometimes encouraging a Little Brother to try a new activity results in a rewarding experience. Tom Hammer recounted the time he introduced his third Little Brother, Sean, to a new activity. "A friend invited us to go water skiing. Sean had never been before, and I'm not all that good either. But we went out anyway and I was able get up and hold on, but Sean didn't want to do it. He was too scared. It was getting late toward dark and we said to him 'This is your last chance,' and he finally said 'OK.' We got him in the water and after a couple of tries, he got up. And he was shocked. His eyes looked so huge and he just hung on, and he just had the biggest grin you've ever seen. He was so happy. So we pulled him around the lake a little bit, and he was so excited about it. Well on the way home, he said to me, 'Tom, you know this is the best day of my life.' You just can't imagine. If we all tried to give somebody the best day of their life, we'd have a much better world."

Introducing a Little Brother to new activities not only provides him with a diverse set of experiences, but in many cases, it develops a new level of self-confidence as well. That self-confidence is then applied to other aspects of a Little Brother's life.

Seek Out-of-the-Ordinary Experiences

As adults, we rarely do things out of the ordinary for fear of what others will think. However, a Big Brother has the opportunity to try new things (or maybe do things he did only as a kid) and at the same time help his Little Brother build self-confidence.

Chuck Crockett, a Big Brother in Framingham, Massachusetts, had always noticed that his Little Brother Gabe took a lot of pride in the activities they did. Chuck liked to emphasize doing things Gabe had never done before. "I wanted him to lose his inhibitions and do something crazy without being stupid," recalls Chuck. Chuck got his chance when they entered the Big Brothers Big Sisters of Middlesex Halloween Contest.

"The first year we were the Jolly Green Giant and the Sprout, and Gabe loved it. We painted ourselves entirely green. Gabe had never just gone out on a limb and done something like that. We even went to McDonald's beforehand and lots of people came up to us. The next year we went as headhunters, and then as Morticia and Uncle Fester the year after that. We won three years in a row. Gabe took a lot of pride in the fact that we won, and he didn't want to go back unless we were the best. We made all the costumes together and didn't have to spend a lot of money."

Doing something out of the ordinary with a Little Brother is often a great relationship builder. It shows a Little Brother that a Big Brother is not only a fun person, but is someone who is confident enough in himself to try new things.

Unforgettable Times

When adults reflect on the best day of their lives, it is usually a memorable event, perhaps with their family or friends. Sometimes that memorable event is an experience that gets passed on. Tom Walsh, a former Little Brother who also became a Big Brother, recalled his first baseball game with his Big Brother, Matt Cashin, some 20 years ago.

"Matt took me to my first Yankees game against the Red Sox. Mom had tried to take us once, but we couldn't get in. Somehow Matt got us in. That day he just told me to bring my glove and my Yankees hat. He said we were going to a park somewhere. I figured we were just going to play catch, so I thought it was no big deal. We kept driving down University Avenue and getting closer to the stadium. Matt even told me we were going to a park that was at the stadium. It wasn't until we were at the gate that I realized what was happening. It was the thrill of my life. Just recently I took my Little Brother to Yankee Stadium for the first time, and what made it so special for me was that Matt was there with us."

Showing a Little Brother a time he will never forget does not mean spending a lot of money. What counts is the thought that gets put into the activity. What a Little Brother will remember is that his Big Brother was thinking especially about him.

Give Back Together

Participating in local events is a great way to develop a Little Brother's sense of community spirit and responsibility. Big Brothers can help Little Brothers see themselves as citizens by providing opportunities for them to make meaningful contributions to their communities. Depending on a Little Brother's level of interest, there are many activities that can be tailored to him.

Some Big Brothers Big Sisters agencies participate in community events like adopt-a-road programs. But there are a lot of other ways to get involved, like volunteering together at a hospital or for a specific event, like Special Olympics. Some matches help their agency by offering to speak together to promote Big Brothers Big Sisters, while other matches have written articles about their experiences for their local papers. Tony and I have done several local cable television appearances to promote our agency. Matches can also offer to help with agency fund-raising events like the annual Bowl For Kid's Sake.

A Big Brother should focus on activities that combine his Little Brother's interests and abilities. Giving back together helps a Little Brother learn more about the world around him, while developing a sense of community and responsibility.

Suggested Activities

There are an endless number of low-cost or free activities to do with a Little Brother. This section highlights just a few of the things Big and Little Brothers do.

Hands-On

Doing hands-on activities with a Little Brother is a great way to spend constructive time together. Additionally, hands-on activities can help a Little Brother feel a sense of accomplishment and pride, which often results in improved self-esteem.

Richard Hlavsa, a 65-year-old Big Brother in Kingston, New York, spends a lot of time doing hands-on activities with his fourth Little Brother, Jonathan, now 10 years old. "We do a lot of gardening. He has his plot of land and I have mine. I also have a pond on my land, and Jonathan decided he wanted to build his own pond. We got a shovel and used that. Then we found a plastic tub, recessed it in the ground, and built a little railing around it. Jonathan put the frogs he had caught in it, and he was very proud of that pond."

Many matches also create their own fun projects. James Johnson, a Big Brother with Chattanooga Big Brothers Big Sisters in Tennessee, took his Little Brother to the library and got a book on how to make a kite. They spent a few hours constructing a huge box kite. The next weekend they went out and flew it. Jim recalls that, "It was wonderful to see the look on James's face because we were flying the kite that *he* built."

Some Big Brothers introduce their Little Brothers to their special interests and hobbies. Tom Bache, a Big Brother in Avondale, Pennsylvania, often works on mechanical things with his Little Brothers. He involves his current Little Brother, Jamie, in one of his pastimes—buying cars, fixing them up, and reselling them. Jamie gets to help paint the cars and hopes to drive one of the cars he and Tom fix up one day.

Other hands-on activities include: model building, garage cleaning, cooking, painting, gardening, car washing, simple mechanical repairs, lawn mowing, and yardwork.

Games

Playing games with a Little Brother can often seem like a fun, entertaining way to spend time. It is also a good opportunity for a Little Brother to apply math and other learning and decision-making skills. Throughout our relationship, Tony and I regularly play Monopoly and other board games. These games force him to use math skills in a fun, nonthreatening environment.

Some possible games include: checkers, board games, cards, darts, jigsaw puzzles, miniature golf, bowling, and billiards.

Sports

Participating in sporting activities is certainly one of the best ways to channel a Little Brother's energy. A Big Brother should find out what sports his Little Brother likes or wants to try. A Big Brother should never push a Little Brother to try something he is not comfortable with. A Big Brother should also remember not to make intensive competition the focus of the activity. A little playful competitiveness is okay, as long as fun and exercise, rather than winning and losing, remain the primary goals.

If a Little Brother plays a team sport, a Big Brother should try whenever possible to attend some of his games. There are also a lot of sporting events that matches can attend for very low cost. Tony and I have often gone to the local YMCA to work out together, swim, and play pickup basketball games.

Some possible sports activities include: hockey/ice skating, roller skating, tennis, baseball, golf, wiffleball, badminton, ping-pong, basketball, football, weight lifting, swimming, and attending professional, minor league, college, and high school sports.

Outdoors

Exploring the outdoors with a Little Brother is a wonderful way to help him develop an appreciation for nature. Gerry Murphy, a former Little Brother and current Big Brother in Topeka, Kansas, credits his Big Brother Matt for spending a lot of time in outdoor activities. "He helped me develop a love for nature. We spent a lot of time boating on the lake with his air force buddies, and we went camping a lot." Even when Matt moved to Arkansas and began a photography career, Gerry visited him during the summers. Gerry remembers traveling around Arkansas with Matt one summer on one of his first photography projects. "I remember he took me to the Buffalo River in the mountains, and we floated down the river and did a lot of exploring and hiking. That summer was the highlight of my childhood." Gerry has been back to that river several times with other people, and a couple of summers ago he took his Little Brother Jason there and had a reunion with Matt.

Exploring the outdoors does not always mean taking trips. It can be as simple as visiting a local park. One of the best things Tony and I do is visit his local park, which he considers a special place, where we fish, play Frisbee, have picnics, and talk. Being outdoors with a Little Brother is often a great escape, for both.

Some possible outdoor activities include: camping, fishing, hiking, bicycling, canoeing, sailing, boating, rafting, tubing, kayaking, skating, cross country skiing, nature walks, local park visits, kite flying, beach outings, mountain climbing, and nature walks.

Supplement School Projects

A Big Brother should show interest in participating with his Little Brother in school projects that require work outside of the classroom. Working with a Little Brother on a school project helps him expand his mind and creativity.

Richard Taylor, a Big Brother in Atlanta, Georgia, saw a dramatic change in his Little Brother, Damon, after working on a tenth grade science fair school project with him. Richard helped Damon build a solar collector, and Damon became fully engaged in the project. With the solar collector, Damon could boil water in 15 seconds and use it to do experiments. Damon won the high school science fair, which qualified him to go to the tri-county fair. He won that and then won the state fair. According to Richard, "It was like a lightbulb went off. For the first time Damon knew he could do whatever he wanted to do. He just needed a challenge."

Some possible projects include: studies (rocks, nature), collecting leaves or shells, weather observation, and projects involving library research.

Hobbies

Exploring new and old hobbies together is another excellent way to build a relationship and learn something new or unique that a Big and Little Brother can share. A Big Brother can discover his Little Brother's interests and find ways to explore them.

Bill Micklitz, a Big Brother in Oshkosh, Wisconsin, learned very early on that he and his Little Brother, Billy, were both "huge Star Trek fans." Last summer Bill and Billy went to their second Star Trek convention in Appleton, Wisconsin.

Some possible hobbies include: model building, photography, card collecting, car shows, and animals.

Eating

Big Brothers who spend enough time with their Little Brothers know that the subject of food eventually comes up. While many Little Brothers probably have their favorite fast food hangouts, Big Brothers can make eating into an adventure as well. A good place to start is the kitchen. Make simple things with a Little Brother like a pizza, and let him select the toppings. Outside of home matches can explore new foods together or even take their favorite foods on a picnic.

Some eating activities: cooking, exploring new foods, making special favorites, and having picnics and cookouts.

Trips and Cultural Activities

There are numerous opportunities to explore new and old parts of the community. Sometimes, simple trips around town provide wonderful memories.

David Brodkin, a Big Brother with the Big Brothers Association of Greater Boston, recalls a memorable time with his Little Brother, Josh. "We were taking a trolley tour through Boston, which Josh was enjoying thoroughly. He particularly liked our second tour guide. He was cracking up hysterically at every ridiculous joke and participated in the audience interaction at every chance. Before we got off, Josh decided to write a letter to the tour guide to show his appreciation. The gist of the note was that he was the greatest and funniest tour guide in the world. We got off in downtown Boston, and Josh handed him the note. As we walked down the sidewalk, I could see that the tour guide had stopped the trolley in the middle of the street to read the note to the packed trolley. The tour resumed, and as it passed us every person on the trolley turned to Josh and waved. It was quite an amusing moment."

Some places to visit include: historical places, museums, day trips (amusement parks, water parks), sightseeing places, and arts-oriented activities like plays or concerts.

Special Interests

Big and Little Brothers will each have a number of special interests to explore. If a Little Brother has a career interest, it can be pursued by visiting someplace associated with that interest. Some matches have visited hospitals, police and fire departments, and even city and town halls. It is important to go beyond "just visiting" and encourage a Little Brother to ask people questions. Matches should let people know who they are and explain the Big Brothers Big Sisters program.

Some special interests to share could include: water sports, radio stations, airports, art fairs, political debates, or job fairs.

Seasonal Events

There are many activities that matches can participate in at certain times of the year. For example, every year Tony and I carve a pumpkin or go apple picking. Holidays are also good times to be creative. Some matches make holiday gifts or cards together.

Some seasonal events (depending on your area): pumpkin carving, apple or berry picking, fairs, Easter egg coloring, Christmas, Chanukah, or other holiday traditions.

Entertainment

Usually there are many enjoyable activities to be found locally by checking the events and activities section of the local paper.

Some local activities include: movies, concerts, circuses, parades, local fairs and festivals, and airplane and balloon shows.

Note: See Appendix III for an extensive list of suggested activities compiled by Big Brothers Big Sisters of Dane County Wisconsin.

Keep Things in Perspective

While Big Brothers want to have enjoyable outings with their Little Brothers, it is important to keep the time spent together in perspective. Big Brother Jeff Venable summarized it best when he said, "The worth that a Little Brother feels comes from you showing up every week, being there, and spending time talking. Nothing miraculous has to happen on any given day, but something spectacular is happening. It's a commitment, but it's a doable commitment, and the upside of it is you learn to have fun and not take life so seriously. And of course it gives you an excuse to go to the park and ride the roller coaster for the fourth time."

chapter

7

One Step at a Time

"My goal when I first got into it was to take a small part of his life and make it very positive. I wasn't going to be able to change his situation, but I knew if I took enough time, together we could make a difference, so that family members and people who knew him six years ago now say they can't believe this is the same kid."

Big Brother Chuck Crockett on his relationship with
his Little Brother Gabe, who recently enlisted in the Marines

≥⊙≤ ≥⊙≤ ≥⊙≤

Big Impact: Dien and Danny[1]

Big Brothers Big Sisters of Sussex County, New Jersey

*Big Brother Dien Wirths has come a long way in his adop-
tive country, the United States, since arriving from Vietnam as a
child. Presently the proprietor of a furniture shop, Dien is achiev-
ing his career aspirations. He understands and appreciates the
direction his life has taken and always works to maximize his
potential.*

*When Dien joined Big Brothers Big Sisters of Sussex County,
he wanted to reciprocate the good fortune he had received. He
wanted to give an underprivileged boy the same opportunities
that were made possible for him. To see a child grow into a successful and productive member of society would be a great
reward for Dien.*

*When he entered the program, 9-year-old Little Brother
Danny was challenging the world. Danny and his mother,
Debby, were experiencing a stressful relationship. Danny, who
had once excelled in academics, had become hostile, belligerent,
and aggressive. Debby believed Danny needed a positive male
role model. She wanted someone who would be understanding
and compassionate, who would listen and care about him, show
interest, and give guidance. Essentially, Debby wanted Danny to
have a friend.*

*When they were first matched in June of 1989, Dien empha-
sized the importance of schoolwork to Danny. Initially, he did not
have much luck encouraging Danny. It took awhile, but eventually Danny's motivation to succeed improved, and so did his
grades. Dien would often do things with Danny to help develop
his mind. Danny now makes the high honor roll regularly with
many A's. Not only did Danny's grades improve, his attitude did
also. The antagonism and anger he once had disappeared. Dien
and Danny mostly did a lot of average activities, like golf, tennis,
and fishing.*

*When Danny was matched with Dien, he not only got a
friend, he got a whole family of support. Danny traveled to Lake*

George every summer with Dien's family. Dien has exposed Danny to many places and people, including his three brothers and his father, Wallace, who himself was a Big Brother in the 1970s. Wallace eventually adopted his Little Brother, Hal, and now calls him his son. Big Brothers Big Sisters runs deep in this family, as Dien's sister-in-law, Debbie, is a Big Sister and an area director with Big Brothers Big Sisters in Philadelphia.

Dien exposed Danny to people in a variety of professions, like policemen and lawyers. But one of the biggest impacts on Danny turned out to be meeting one of Dien's brothers, Phuong, a doctor. Danny was so struck by visiting Phuong at the hospital that he decided he wanted to become a doctor himself. This was not just a passing phase for Danny. By his sophomore year in high school in 1995, Danny was choosing classes—like Biology— that would develop his interest in medicine. Danny made an effort to read anything and everything he could that would help. According to his mom, "Danny cleaned out the local library. You just can't give him enough to learn." For his efforts, Dien was named the Big Brother of the Year by Big Brothers Big Sisters of Sussex County.

Being a Big Brother has had a tremendous impact on Dien. "Having a Little Brother like Danny has given me a marvelous opportunity to observe firsthand what boyhood is like in America. As a youth in Vietnam, I experienced none of the pleasures that are almost automatic for American kids. In Asia, a boy is put to work almost as soon as he can walk and talk, because the nations there are so poor that every family member must produce in some way. Doing things, playing sports, and going places with Danny have given me a better concept of life here in the United States. At the same time, it has given me an adult sense of responsibility as I attempt to help a youngster develop into a young man who will be able to meet successfully some of the many difficult challenges we all face as we move into maturity. Being a Big Brother to Danny has had many fun moments, but it has also been a sobering and satisfying experience."

Debby gratefully acknowledges the impact that Dien and his family had on her son. A couple of years ago she wrote a letter that expressed her feelings.

"Many years ago I sent my shy quiet son off with a stranger. Never had he been away from me. Who would have guessed my

Danny's life was to change forever on that sunny June day? Dien came into Dan's life when he was desperately needed. Dan was a reclusive child without ambition. Nintendo® was his whole life. School work wasn't important. Dien has given him self-esteem to change his whole life into a dream come true. Dan not only got a Big Brother, he got a whole big family. Each and every member of this family regards Dan with respect and he returns those feelings back. They have all given Danny a reason to succeed. He lives to fill their eyes and hearts with pride of his achievements. Dan's match was made in heaven. Our greatest day will be to see 'Dr. Dan' graduate. Thank you Dien and all. My Dan will be a great man through your love."[2]

Dien and Danny, two people who never would have crossed paths, now are the best of friends together, making a Big Impact.

=◎= =◎= =◎=

The Match Process[3]

A Big Brothers Big Sisters match is carefully administered and supported by rigorous standards and trained personnel. Big Brothers Big Sisters staff strive for matches that are not only safe and suited to the child's needs but also harmonious and built to last.

Children are referred to a Big Brothers Big Sisters agency from a variety of sources, including schools and social service agencies. Usually it is the parent or guardian who makes the initial contact. When a child is referred to the program, a caseworker typically meets with the parent or guardian and gives them information about the agency's services. Children considered for matches typically must be between 6 and 14 years of age at the time of application. With few exceptions these children are from either single-parent or nonparent (i.e. live with relatives or in foster care) homes.

An interview is done in the parent's or guardian's home to get as much family history as possible and detail regarding behavior, school performance, interests, and any problems or issues the child is experiencing. Agency staff get to know the child and his or her family, carefully noting likes, dislikes, temperament, interests, age, and personality. The child is told about the program, and staff learn about the child's interests. Once the interview is completed, the child is added to the waiting list for a Big Brother.

Little Brothers and Their Families

Little Brothers range in age from 5 to 18 years old, although the typical age range when a Little Brother is first matched is 6 to 14 years old. Little Brothers come from all social, financial, and ethnic backgrounds. Some are having trouble at home or school. For others, the biggest problem is loneliness. Little Brothers often need to learn about trust, develop problem-solving skills, and experience life beyond their own neighborhoods. Little Brothers usually come from father-absent homes, and need someone with whom to identify. Many of the boys, for a variety of reasons, are at greater risk for the negative influences of society, whether drug, alcohol use, or other factors, such as dropping out of school. For example, at the Big Brothers Association of Greater Boston, 85 percent of Little Brothers are boys with low self-confidence or poor social skills, 70 percent are underachievers in school, and 50 percent are at risk of dropping out of school.[4]

Living Situation

Of the boys in the Big Brothers Big Sisters program—those currently matched and on the waiting list—more than 82 percent live with one parent, while about 6 percent live with two parents. The remainder live with other relatives, in group homes, foster homes, or other arrangements. Approximately 48 percent of Little Brothers' and Little Sisters' families receive some form of income assistance.

Race

More than two-thirds of boys enrolled in Big Brothers Big Sisters programs—both matched and unmatched—are Caucasian, and about 24 percent are African-American. Close to 7 percent are Hispanic, and the remainder of the boys are Asian, Pacific Islander, Native American, and other races.

Length of Wait

Currently, slightly more than 51 percent of boys wait a year or less to be matched, while more than 34 percent of waiting Little Brothers wait for two years or longer. Astonishingly, nearly 10 percent of boys have been waiting four years or longer for a Big Brother.[5]

The Volunteer Intake Process

Because the Big Brothers Big Sisters program matches an unrelated adult in an unchaperoned one-to-one relationship with a child, agencies focus on safety and commitment issues during the volunteer screening process. This process is exceptionally effective, with all Big Brothers Big Sisters agencies drawing guidance from a uniform set of standards and procedures. The Big Brothers Big Sisters professional infrastructure helps maximize the chance that a Big Brothers Big Sisters relationship will take root and flourish.

Big Brothers Big Sisters agencies require volunteers to complete an application, attend an orientation, pass a criminal records check, submit the names of several references, participate in a personal interview, undergo a home assessment, and attend a training session. Some agencies also administer psychological tests and check driving records. The goal of this process is to help agencies identify safe and committed volunteers and screen out those who are inappropriate. Through this process, the agency gets a sense of the volunteer, while the volunteer learns about the agency and what it means to be a Big Brother or Big Sister. While each agency may have slight variations to the volunteer intake process, it is basically the same throughout the country.

What to Expect at First Contact

A prospective volunteer typically calls his local agency to express an interest in becoming a Big Brother. Agency staff describe the program, the basic eligibility criteria, and the required time commitment. Basic eligibility criteria typically include: a minimum age requirement (usually 18 to 21), access to transportation, no current substance abuse problems, acceptable driving record, and safe personal record (e.g., no felony assault convictions). Some agencies also have residency requirements (length of time in an area) and employment requirements. Other important factors, such as understanding of children and status of other family and personal relationships, are usually addressed when an individual expresses interest in learning more about the program. If an individual meets the basic requirements and remains interested, he is encouraged to attend an orientation and/or complete an application.

The Orientation

Most agencies have a group orientation session where interested individuals can learn about the different programs they offer. Some agencies require attendance at an orientation before an application is submitted. These group sessions generally last about an hour. Potential volunteers hear a history of the agency, an outline of the screening procedures, and some of the agency policies and practices. They learn what is and what is not expected of them. Usually a Big is there to share his volunteer story. Prospective volunteers get to hear firsthand experiences that help them get a sense of what a match is like and the types of activities they might do. Prospects are able to ask any questions they may have and talk with agency staff about the various programs. There is no obligation whatsoever. Prospects decide what is best for them, and the agency helps them reach a decision. Attending an orientation is a good way to learn about the work a local agency is doing and how it impacts the community.

The Application

Every agency requires volunteers to complete an application with their address, race, age, current employment, criminal history, and names and addresses of references. References may include an employer, relative, significant other, or other people who have known the applicant well for at least a few years. When agencies receive an application, agency staff collect data from references and submit the applicant's name to legal and motor vehicle agencies for background checks.

Criminal and Driving Records Check

As part of the screening process, applicants authorize the agency to conduct a criminal records check. All agencies exclude individuals who have committed violent crimes, crimes against a person, or sexual crimes. Some agencies also conduct a motor vehicles check to uncover any unsafe driving records that might pose a risk to a child.

Interview and Home Assessment

All prospective volunteers are carefully interviewed, and a thorough inquiry is done to ensure that they are reliable, caring adults. This interview is bit personal in nature, but the questions that are asked of everyone are intended to ensure the safety of the children.

The interview, which typically lasts one to two hours, is the best opportunity for agencies to really get to know the applicant. Some topics discussed might include: motivation for applying; understanding of the commitment required; marital or dating situation; family background and relationships with family members; drug and alcohol use; and hobbies.

The primary goal of the interview is to determine whether applicants pose a safety risk to a child or are unlikely to honor their commitment. The interview also helps provide information the agency can use in making a match.

A key part of the screening process is an in-depth interview conducted by a youth worker in the applicant's home so it, too, can be checked out as safe for a child. "The assessment is where we find out about the history and the background of the volunteer to learn about his lifestyle, his experiences, and how they might impact his volunteer experience as a role model. We also look at the safety issues as they relate to the child," says John Hamilton, executive director of the Big Brothers Big Sisters Association of Columbus and Franklin County in Ohio. "We feel it is very important that we assess the appropriateness of the volunteer and that, secondly, we look at the skills and capabilities that volunteer has to offer a child so we can make the best match possible. Thus we're not only screening out those individuals deemed inappropriate but looking at the skills and knowledge base of the ones we accept as to how they might best be able to help a child. Then we try to find the child who fits that volunteer's strengths most closely."[6]

The Next Steps

When the interview and background checks have been completed, the caseworker assigned to evaluate the prospective volunteer writes up a report that includes a recommendation to accept or reject the applicant. Typically the report is reviewed by a staff screening committee after checking the file for thoroughness and consistency. In some agencies the final decision is made by a group, while in other agencies, management staff make the decision. In some agencies the decision is left to case managers, depending on their experience level.

When a Volunteer Is Accepted

When a volunteer is accepted he will meet with a caseworker to hear profiles of Littles on the waiting list with whom the caseworker thinks the volunteer would be compatible. Volunteers choose the Little Brother with whom they would like to be matched. The parent or guardian and potential Little Brother are then made aware of the volunteer's profile. If the parent or guardian and Little Brother approve the volunteer's profile, a meeting is set up with the caseworker and volunteer to meet the Little Brother and his family. And then the real fun begins.

Many potential Big Brothers have a difficult time choosing a Little Brother. There are many factors that a prospective volunteer can evaluate: location of the Little, interests, age, and length of time on the waiting list. Some people prefer to live closer to their Little; others do not mind a short drive. There are no right or wrong answers, and caseworkers help guide prospective volunteers through the decision-making process.

Caseworker Support

When a volunteer has chosen a Little Brother and the match is confirmed, the volunteer is assigned to a caseworker. The caseworker is there to help the volunteer with all match issues. The caseworker keeps in regular contact with the parent, child, and volunteer to ensure the relationship is developing satisfactorily. If any difficulties should develop in the friendship, the caseworker tries to be of assistance in working these out. In addition, the caseworker may counsel the child or parent if they have any concerns, or may refer them to professional community agencies for help. All information about the child and family is kept confidential; however, the caseworker cooperates with the schools, courts, and family agencies in the interest of the child and with the permission of the parent. All relevant information on the child and the family is shared with the volunteer. It is essential that the volunteer respects the importance of confidentiality.

The caseworker is available to encourage and support the volunteer in his efforts. Typically, a caseworker follows up with the volunteer monthly in the first year and quarterly after that.

Training and Services

Many Big Brothers Big Sisters agencies have a training seminar for newly accepted volunteers. The training helps volunteers learn the stages of development that their Littles might go through. The training helps teach relationship building and communication skills. Some agencies also offer ongoing training, including courses that Bigs can take with their Littles.

Most agencies have a periodic newsletter for volunteers and parents highlighting current recreational, educational, and cultural activities and events for matches. Occasionally agencies receive donated tickets to entertainment and sports events that are distributed to matches. Agencies also have other outings and holiday events in which matches can participate.

A Final Word on the Matching Process[7]

This process, which is done for every prospective volunteer, is essential to ensuring that every child is matched with a safe, caring adult. Mothers and guardians who so courageously open their children's lives up to other adults depend on the Big Brothers Big Sisters agencies to ensure their children's safety. They should expect no less. The screening process done by Big Brothers Big Sisters is considered one of the most thorough and complete of all mentoring programs. Everything that is asked of prospective volunteers is done with the child's safety and security in mind.

The results of such strong protocols are participants who are willing and anxious to work together. "The unique thing about our program," says John Hamilton, "is that nobody is forced upon us willfully and that makes a big difference for all the participants. The kids are here because they want to participate; parents want them involved because they see the benefits. And the volunteers are here because they want to help the kids. The important thing is to obtain the best possible match in each case."

Big Brothers Big Sisters agencies develop match programs based on their local environments. In addition to the "core match" of one Big Brother or Big Sister to a Little Brother or Little Sister, couples matches, cross-gender matches, school-based mentoring, high school and college mentoring, and community-specific mentoring are available in some areas.

The Core Match Program

The traditional match is a one-to-one relationship. Boys who are 6 to 14 years old are matched with carefully screened mentors. Matches spend almost all of their time together in an unsupervised, unstructured manner. They choose the time, the place, and what to do together. Paramount to this environment is the screening that Big Brothers Big Sisters provides and the initial training. The agency also facilitates the match and the ongoing relationship, and makes sure that staff members are always there to help out with questions or in a crisis.

Couples Matches

Many agencies are beginning to expand the mentoring philosophy to two adults per child. This program functions in the same way as the traditional match, but allows for a two-to-one relationship where a couple, typically a husband and wife, goes on most outings together with the Little Brother or Sister. The program was developed in response to the increasingly limited time that individuals and their significant others have. The screening requirements are the same as the traditional match. Even in couples matches there is a notable amount of one-to-one time spent together with the child, as often one adult has more availability. There are currently about 1,800 such matches in the country.

Cross-Gender Matches

Some agencies are now beginning cross-gender matches, primarily Big Sisters with Little Brothers. The fact is that many agencies have more Big Sister volunteers than Big Brother volunteers, and have more Little Brothers waiting for a match, so they match Little Brothers whose parents/guardians approve of a Big Sister match.

There are instances where there is an advantage to a boy forming a role-model relationship with a woman. Some of the boys in the program live in mother-absent homes. Many have lived without mothering for most of their lives. If a boy is willing to try a Big Sister, his odds of getting matched quickly are better than the often one-year to three-year wait for a Big Brother. Agencies carefully match interests, likes, and dislikes. Currently there are approximately 1,400 cross-gender matches.

School-Based Mentoring

Some agencies have a school mentoring program where mentors are asked to share one hour a week with a child who is in elementary school during the academic year. Each mentor is matched with a child who would benefit from some extra attention. The mentor may do tutoring work with the child, but matches can also spend the time talking or doing other activities.

High School and College Programs

Some agencies utilize high school and college students as mentors. These programs are similar to the traditional match program, although volunteers are mostly only required to make a commitment during the school year.

Community-Specific Mentoring

Some agencies have programs tailored to specific cultures, which aim to match children, many of whom are new to their community, with adults of similar backgrounds. The intent is to help the children get a better grasp of their communities and cultural heritages.

Other agencies also have programs tailored to specific needs, such as children of parents with HIV or AIDS, or children with terminal illnesses. This type of program requires a volunteer who feels emotionally prepared to work with children in these cases. The aim of this program is to help children through difficult transition periods and to help improve the quality of life. Greg Jones had been doing volunteer work with the MAP AIDS project in Charlotte, North Carolina, when he decided to become a Big Brother through the Big Brothers Big Sisters Division of United Family Services. For the past five years Greg has been a Big Brother to a boy whose family members were dying of AIDS. Greg says that in these situations, "The main thing is to get a child away from his situation for a little while and to provide support when a parent or family member dies."

Other Services

Program services vary by agency and not all agencies provide all of these services. It is best to check with the local agency about their specific types of volunteer and service programs.

chapter

8

Living the Commitment

"By the time I was 20, most of my friends were either dead or

in jail. The reason I was not in one of these groups was because

I had a Big Brother. My Big Brother taught me the importance

of education, working hard, and obeying the law. My Big

Brother also showed me what a healthy, stable family can

mean to a young boy growing up."

Kenny Ross, former Little Brother back in 1940, who went on
to co-found Big Brothers Big Sisters of Greater Pittsburgh

Big Impact:
Darrell Hill and Luther Alston[1]

Youth Visions Inc., Cleveland, Ohio

A little support and encouragement often go a long way in life. For some boys, it can be the difference between making it and being written off. Such was the case for Darrell Hill. Darrell grew up in the East Woodhill Estates housing projects in Cleveland with his mother and brother. Darrell, who never knew his father, was having a difficult time with school, often talking back to his teachers. He had to repeat the second grade. Darrell's elementary school principal told him he was a loser and that he would never make it, let alone go to college.

When he was 12, Darrell got a Big Brother. When his Big Brother was not able to spend a lot of time with him, in stepped Luther Alston, the Little Buddy/Big Buddy coordinator for Youth Visions, to help "fill in the gaps." Darrell and Luther often went fishing on Luther's boat and worked together on Luther's car. They also did a lot simple things around the house, like cutting the lawn, and replacing windows and screen doors.

According to Darrell, he was suspended from John Hay High School "every other week." He stole a car once, and Luther was there to make sure he did not go to jail. When he was 16, Darrell worked at a gas station and was falsely accused of stealing money. Luther stepped in to make sure charges were never pressed against him. Darrell failed the eleventh grade, more or less left school after that, and got a job washing dishes. He got fired from that job, but Luther was there to help him get a job as a janitor at a veteran's hospital.

Soon afterwards Darrell decided he had to make a change. "I didn't want to be just another person washing dishes or mopping floors my whole life." So he went back to school and got busy. He got interested in drama, did some plays, and ran the stage. He started writing for the school newspaper. For Darrell, "It was almost like going to school for the first time. My body had been there, but never my mind." Darrell entered a speech contest and won a partial college scholarship. On a bet with a friend, Darrell took a sewing class. He ended up learning to sew and getting another scholarship after entering a clothing contest.

Throughout their friendship, Luther never condemned Darrell. Darrell was always afraid he was letting Luther down, and Luther would always reassure him with words like, "No you didn't let me down. You just made a mistake that's all." To Darrell, Luther was a lifesaver.

"Luther was always there when I was getting in trouble, lending a helping hand and telling me basically what I was doing wrong. It never failed that when something went wrong he was always there for me. When I think back on those times, it was like Luther saw something in me that said, 'There must something good in this kid, we just need to find it and make him realize it.' And that's why I'm here today, because I know I was hanging with the wrong crowd and I know that had he not been around, and with my mom being a single parent, I probably would have wound up in jail if not dead. There's no doubt in my mind."

Darrell went on to Kent State University and got interested in television and film production. He met a producer who worked for a PBS affiliate and got the opportunity to work there. Since then he has worked for NBC in New York and has produced a couple of television documentaries in Cleveland. Today that "loser" is an independent producer/director and news videographer. He now works for a television station in Orlando, Florida, but has dreams of working for Universal or Disney.

Luther is extremely proud of Darrell. A few years ago, he remembers seeing Darrell just before he left for Florida. "I know I couldn't have felt better about my own son," recalled Luther. Luther, who has been involved with Youth Vision since 1972, is as energized today about working with kids like Darrell as he ever was. "It's because of kids like Darrell that I'm still doing what I do."

Darrell feels the same way about Luther. He refers to Luther as the "Martin Luther King of Youth Visions." He believes that kids today just need direction and support like he had. "The key was spending time with me. Luther, his wife, and his son all treated me like a part of their family. I really had no direction and was being pulled from the bad elements. And if you don't have someone showing you right from wrong, then ultimately you're going to be the victim. But Luther was there for me. Words can't express enough what he did for me. I may not have survived life today as I know it if it weren't for Luther Alston."

Luther knows that more men need to come forward as Big Brothers. He believes that men need to understand that being a Big Brother is not as much work as they might think. "What kids need—time and encouragement—hasn't changed. We all have something to give, and we have all been given gifts to work with. If you fail to use those gifts, you are only doing your-self a disservice."

Fortunately for Darrell Hill and many other boys in the Youth Visions program, Luther Alston is still there, everyday, making a Big Impact.

No Magic Formula

When a man first becomes a Big Brother, he has all sorts of ideas and expectations about how his relationship with his Little Brother should develop. While being a Big Brother is not the most difficult thing a man can ever do, it is not something to be taken lightly. There is no magic formula that will guarantee success. However, when a man remains committed to being a positive influence in his Little Brother's life, many good things will result.

This chapter offers some suggestions on how to develop a good relationship with a Little Brother. Part of the advice comes directly from guidelines given by Big Brothers Big Sisters programs. In addition I will share with you some of the things that have worked for me in supporting Tony, and draw upon many of the experiences of the Big and Little Brothers I interviewed.

Simple practices help Big Brothers make the best use of the gifts they have to share. By following these practices, Little Brothers will be more open to realizing and sharing many of the gifts they have. When this occurs, the result is often gratifying relationships for both Bigs and Littles.

Have Realistic Expectations

Big Brothers come into the program with a tremendous amount of enthusiasm. They get involved to have an impact on a boy's life and to be agents of change in a boy's future. However, it is important to remember that significant change is not something that occurs overnight. The impact a Big Brother would like to make will be realized through a process of life events and experiences that occur *over time.* The length of time it takes to see any noticeable change varies with each Little Brother. In some matches Big Brothers or mothers see improvements after only a few months, while in other matches, changes are not seen for many years.

Significant long-term change in a Little Brother's life is not something over which a Big Brother, as one person, has control. Ultimately, the decisions and choices each Little Brother makes are his. Marc Freedman, author of *The Kindness of Strangers,* aptly reminds us that, "If you expect to waltz into someone's life and immediately transform it, you will be in for quite a shock."[2] Even Big Brothers in very close relationships with their Little Brothers discover that they are only one influence among many. I often feel limited by what I can accomplish with Tony, given all the other influences he is exposed to daily. I realize that I must not allow myself to concentrate on what I *cannot* accomplish. Instead, I focus on the little things I can do that will ensure that I am the best unconditionally caring, supportive, and loving friend I can be. I understand that I alone cannot solve the whole puzzle, but I can be one solid piece that helps lead toward completing a clearer picture.

Bill Sheil, a news anchor for WEWS in Cleveland, Ohio, and Big Brother to Jamie for more than three years through Youth Visions Inc., has this advice for other Bigs: "You can't go in and say you're going to fix something. The idea that you are going to spend a few hours a week with a child and *fix something,* well the parents would laugh at you. You shouldn't go into it thinking that if their life isn't better as a result of your friendship that you have failed. If you have made a child smile some and brought some joy, then you're a success. And who's to say what his life, or yours for that matter, will be like in 20 years? Just try to bring a little bit of joy into each other's lives every week. If any more than that happens, then that's great."

Not trying to bring about major change overnight is a good practice. If a Big Brother looks at the relationship with a long view, he will see that creating a good friendship is a gradual process that builds over time.

Keep in Regular Contact

Consistency is the best first step toward earning a Little Brother's trust. Visibly being in his life on a regular basis is an important building block of friendship. Whatever amount of time a Big Brother has committed, it is essential to honor that commitment, even if some of it is by phone.

A Big Brother should initiate contact and conversations with his Little Brother. He should not wait for his Little Brother to come to him. A good match begins with the Big Brother taking the lead. A Little Brother needs to know that his Big Brother will continue to seek him out. After each outing, a Big Brother should reassure his Little Brother by discussing when they are going to see each other or talk on the phone. A Big Brother should leave little room for doubt as to when and if his Little Brother is going to see him again.

Jeff Lambrecht, a Big Brother in Detroit, Michigan, has seen the impact that consistency has on his Little Brother Jack. "At first I'd come over and he wouldn't be there, because he wasn't expecting me to be there, so he wasn't going to plan his day around it. But I always let him know I'm going to call him every week and when we're going to get together. I always am where I say I'm going to be, so he's learned he can count on me being there. Now he's always there when I show up."

In addition, a Big Brother should encourage his Little Brother to call him at home or work, if calling at work is allowed. A Little Brother and his mother or guardian should know the best times to reach the Big Brother at home or at work. A Big Brother should not be discouraged if it takes some time before his Little Brother feels comfortable calling him. Just because a Little Brother does not call does not mean he is not thinking about his Big Brother. Often just knowing he *can* call his Big Brother provides the Little Brother with an important sense of security.

Be on Time and Do Not Break Appointments

So many Little Brothers have been stood up by friends and relatives that they often enter into a relationship with an iron guard around their hearts, with the expectation of being forgotten or set aside for more important events. A Big Brother who befriends one of these boys and extends the simple courtesy of being where he says he will be provides his Little Brother with an unspoken, deeply felt sense of security and value.

Chuck Crockett, a Big Brother in Norwood, Massachusetts, with Big Brothers Big Sisters of South Middlesex, told me how he earned his Little Brother Gabe's trust. "I did things to make sure he trusted me, like when I said I was going to be there at a certain time. He told me he would wait by the clock. If I was supposed to be there at 11:00, the first thing out of his mouth when I got there was 'Oh you were here at 10:59 or 10:57 or 11:01.' So I just realized the significance of it to him. As a result of being on time, he trusted me almost immediately."

Little things like showing up on time can have great significance to a Little Brother. Big Brothers should understand this and accept the importance attached to it. In this instance, Chuck was successful because he accepted that time was important to Gabe, and he made sure to be on time every time.

A Big Brother should never stand his Little Brother up. Children have long memories. A Little Brother counts on his Big Brother being there so a Big Brother should not disappoint his Little Brother. Big Brothers should do what they promise and live up to their bargains. A Big Brother should not give a Little Brother any reason to think that he might be like others who have disappointed him in the past.

Establish a Rapport with the Mother or Guardian

Many of the mothers and guardians who have placed their boys in the Big Brothers Big Sisters program have done so courageously. They realize the benefit of having a support system and special friend for their son. While most are excited when their child is matched, there can still be some anxiety and concern on their part. A Big Brother should remember that this is a new experience for everyone involved, but there are things he can do to put the mother or guardian at ease.

Be certain to get approval for outings. If the Little Brother is very young, the Big Brother may want to talk with the mother directly. If the situation is appropriate, a Big Brother may have his Little Brother ask his mother. Either way, it is important that a Big Brother makes sure what he and his Little Brother do has the mother's approval and that her concerns are addressed. It is also important for a Big Brother to make sure he lets his Little Brother's mother or guardian know when the Little Brother will return from outings. If a Big Brother knows he is going to be late, he should call the mother and let her know.

A Big Brother should take the time to learn any important information about his Little Brother, such as medical or health information. He should also make sure to know how to reach the mother or guardian in case of emergency.

These simple courtesies will go a long way toward helping ease any anxiety and fear that mothers or guardians may have. Respecting the Little Brother's mother or guardian is a good opportunity to model good behavior and show support for the family unit.

Avoid Over-Involvement

A Big Brother should always show concern for his Little Brother and his Little Brother's family, but he should not become over-involved in family issues. A Big Brother should remember that he is there solely to support his Little Brother and should avoid trying to deal with anything more than that. There is a tendency to think a Big Brother can objectively step in and help resolve difficult situations. The reality is that a Big Brother can end up getting involved over his head, which will directly impact the match.

If a Big Brother sees situations that need professional assistance, he should discuss these matters with his caseworker or suggest that the mother or guardian call the Big Brothers Big Sisters office. Staff members have many years of experience working with families. They can offer suggestions or help refer the family to the appropriate resources.

When issues do arise, it is important for a Big Brother to be supportive of the parent, even when he might disagree. A Big Brother needs to remember that the mother or guardian has ultimate responsibility for the child. The Big Brother should avoid getting caught in the middle of issues. If a Big Brother strongly disagrees with something, he should discuss it with his caseworker.

George and Betty Munroe, a couples match with Big Brothers Big Sisters of Charlotte County when they lived in Punta Gorda, Florida, have this advice for Bigs: "We like to think of ourselves as an extension of family and friends. You must be careful not to give the mother the appearance of taking any affection away from her. We always honor her and hold her in high regard. With our Little Brother, Brett, we made a birthday party for her, and we always remember Mother's Day and celebrate Christmas. We try to show that we all deserve to be loved equally." George, 79, and Betty, 65, have been supportive of Brett's mother since their match began more than ten years ago.

A Big Brother should avoid discussing his Little Brother with the mother in the boy's presence. This can create conflict and unease for the Little Brother. He may feel betrayed and lose the sense that his Big Brother is there for him, which will directly impact the match. If it is beneficial to discuss a Little Brother's progress with his mother or guardian, the Big Brother should try reaching her by phone or arranging a time to talk when his Little Brother is at school or involved in some other activity.

The basic rule of thumb to follow is to keep the focus of the relationship on the Little Brother. A Big Brother should work with the Little Brother's mother or guardian where needed to help support the relationship with him.

Do Not Try to Be a Problem Solver

When children have problems, we often go into a "crisis management" mode. We naturally want to help, and since we have more life experience, we immediately want to give them the answers and tell them what they should do. Rather than trying to solve a problem for a Little Brother, a Big Brother can be most supportive by helping a Little Brother work through issues and solve his own problems. More often than not, a Big Brother's best role is to ask questions, be a sounding board, and give feedback. Most children only see one solution or resolution to issues. But the more questions a Big Brother asks, the more it makes a Little Brother think about other possible alternatives. Asking questions and letting a Little Brother come to his own conclusions help develop critical thinking and problem-solving skills, teach patience, and reinforce the importance of consequences. Most importantly, this encourages a Little Brother to take responsibility and ownership for his decisions.

At the beginning of a match, a Big Brother should get to know his Little Brother gradually and at a pace that is comfortable for him. While a Big Brother may want his Little Brother to express his thoughts and feelings, the Little Brother may not feel comfortable yet. A Big Brother should not expect to be an immediate sounding board. This type of communication will occur only after a relationship has been established and a boy feels comfortable sharing his concerns.

A couple of years ago I had a situation with Tony that taught me the importance of letting him make his own decisions. It was late in the evening when the phone rang. I could tell by the anxious tone of his voice that something was wrong. Tony's home and school situations were weighing on him. He seemed extremely stressed and angry, and he concluded that his only option was to run away for a little while.

I have learned over time the importance of validating Tony's feelings. More often than not he simply wants to be heard, understood, and not judged. Rather than rush to judgment or offer solutions, I really listened to what Tony had to say. He clearly needed to vent his frustrations, and I told him it was okay to feel the way he did.

At this point I began to discuss the options with him. I could not tell Tony what to do, but I could ask him the right questions and give him enough information to make a good, rational decision. I asked Tony a series of questions about what would happen if he did run away, what his family's reaction would be, how it would affect his ability to see me, and other possible outcomes. The first couple of questions Tony had figured out, but as I asked him more about the possible consequences, he seemed to realize that punishment, less freedom, and loss of family trust would play a big part.

The next question I asked Tony opened another door for me. I asked if this was something that he might still be upset over tomorrow, next week, or even a month from now. He was unsure of the answer to that, and so I posed one final thought to him. I asked him, "Since you are not sure how long you are going to be upset for, and you know what might happen if you run away, don't you deserve to sleep on it tonight and see if you feel the same way tomorrow? That's what I would do." Tony agreed one more night would not hurt. I, in turn, made him promise to call me the next day if he still felt the same way. By doing so, I assured him that I was still his friend no matter what decision he made.

By late afternoon the next day, I had not heard from Tony. I called his house to see if he was home from school and much to my relief, he was. I asked him how he was feeling, and he told me that he was not as upset anymore. I could tell just from the tone of his voice that things were different. Happily, his main concern was when we were getting together next.

Since then the issue of running away has never come up. This experience reinforced for me that my role is to listen to Tony's concerns and help him explore the options and consequences, good and bad. It is empowering to a child when you say, "What do you think?" Even if a Big Brother knows what direction is right, he can lead his Little Brother to the answer by asking the right questions. A Big

Brother can help his Little Brother solve problems by asking: What is the situation? What have you done so far? What else can you do? What is your next step? These four questions let a Little Brother know that he shares the responsibility for solving his own problems. When he feels like he has made the decision, it helps teach him that he can take control of many aspects of his life. When problems arise, effective Big Brothers resist telling their Little Brothers what to do and instead work together to jointly address the issue.

Listen, Listen, Listen

One of the best ways for a Little Brother to take himself seriously is for his Big Brother to take him seriously. A Big Brother should spend a lot of time simply listening to his Little Brother, determining what his Little's interests are, and asking him questions about those interests.

Children divulge a lot when they speak. A Big Brother should watch for the meaning behind his Little Brother's words and actions. Is he gloomy or depressed? Is he angry about something? Have things gone wrong at home or school? A Big Brother should be aware of danger signs. If something seems to be bothering a Little Brother, a Big Brother can ask what is hurting him. A Big Brother should suffer along with his Little Brother by empathizing. For a Little Brother, just having someone who will listen is often a tremendous help.

Bob Chiappinelli, a Big Brother six times through Big Brothers of Rhode Island and a reporter for the *Providence Journal-Bulletin* for more than 31 years, described how important listening was to one of his former Little Brothers, Paul. "Paul called me one night when he was 16, and I could tell he was agitated. He described to me a particularly bad day where he had gotten into a confrontation, which was unusual for him. He labored in the telling and I knew it was an effort. I felt good that he trusted me. When he finished, I said 'Wow, it sounds like it's been a bummer for you.' I could hear a sigh of relief from him. Later I wondered if I would have as readily tuned in that way with my children. More than likely, I would have lectured and lost their interest."

A Big Brother should make a sincere effort to understand how his Little Brother is feeling. He should put himself in his Little Brother's shoes and think of how he would have reacted to what his Little Brother is going through. A Big Brother must remember he is not there to solve his Little Brother's problems. He can help his Little Brother understand and process issues.

Mike Propp, a Big Brother in Manhattan, Kansas, with Big Brothers Big Sisters of Sedgwick County, says a key to building trust with his third Little Brother, Charles, was listening. "I listened to him a lot and didn't tell him what to do or what was right or wrong. I just gave him the feeling that there was always somebody there he could talk to. As a result, Charles opened up a lot and came out of his shell." Now, 11 years after they were matched, Charles is 19 and out of high school. Mike is still there to listen to Charles's concerns about life.

A Big Brother should remember that a Little Brother usually has a reason for acting the way he does. Inappropriate behaviors usually reflect a misguided attempt to feel better about himself and his situation. While Little Brothers need to be held accountable for their actions, it is necessary to look behind their behaviors.

Recast Problems as Learning Opportunities

When children are having a difficult time with something, they often focus on the negative aspects of the issue. A Big Brother can help his Little Brother see the other side. Again, without telling him all the answers, a Big Brother can reframe all problems as opportunities for growth. No matter how negative the circumstance, there is always some potential for learning and growth. By reframing problems, Big Brothers can teach Little Brothers to handle conflict better and respect alternate points of view. For example, one Big Brother I talked with recounted a story where his Little Brother dealt with what he perceived to be a racial slur. The Little Brother was playing basketball with his Big Brother when their ball went over to another court. An African-American child threw the ball back, calling the Little Brother, who was Caucasian, a name he did not like. Later, when the other boy's ball went into the Little Brother's court, the Little Brother threw the ball back and called a name back. Even though retaliation was not the best result here, there was a set of opportunities for learning.

In this instance, the Little Brother thought there was only one option, to return the favor of an insult. His Big Brother, though, took the time to discuss the situation with him. The Big Brother asked what else he could have done and if he understood what consequences his actions might have had.

While a Big Brother cannot convince or tell a Little Brother how to think or act, he can make him aware of other choices. But often awareness alone is not enough. A Big Brother can help a Little Brother understand that if other choices are put into action, those choices will help him achieve more of what he really wants. In many cases, Little Brothers, deep down, want things like acceptance and respect. If a Big Brother discusses more effective ways of helping a Little Brother get what he wants, the Little Brother may act differently the next time a situation arises.

Do Not Crowd

Little Brothers who are wary of adult male relationships may initially need to keep a certain "safe" distance. Not surprisingly, when Bigs try to enthusiastically fashion relationships with these types of boys, their attempts often fail. This is not because the Bigs do not try hard enough, but because they try *too hard*. A Big Brother should simply respect a Little Brother's need for space, just as he would want his own space respected. Sometimes, at the very time a strong relationship is emerging, a Little Brother may need to back off a bit. A Big Brother should not interpret this as a failure but as a temporary adjustment. A Little Brother sometimes gives subtle signs of how he feels. He may give no direct feedback to his Big Brother, but he may talk openly about his Big Brother to his mother or guardian.

I try to make sure that I always give Tony the space he needs. When he appears to be troubled, I have an urge to have him tell me everything that is going on. Instead of pushing him to talk about things that may be uncomfortable, I ask him how he is doing and ask if there is anything going on that he wants to talk about. When he does not want to talk, I just reinforce that I am always there if he ever wants to, and if he does not, I accept that. What I have found is that by not putting pressure on him to talk, Tony will often call me later or talk with me the next time I see him.

A Big Brother does not have to be a professional counselor in order to make a Little Brother feel safe with him. He should find a quiet time and place to listen to his Little Brother. Often all a Big Brother needs to ask are questions like, "Is anything bothering you? Would you like to talk about it? Is there anything I can do to help?" But a Big Brother should also be careful to respect his Little Brother's boundaries and privacy. A Big Brother should not initiate conversations about personal matters, especially uncomfortable family matters that a Little Brother may not be proud of, unless his Little Brother brings them up.

Big Brothers do best when they work with their Little Brothers at a pace with which their Littles are comfortable. Big Brothers must accept their Little Brothers and value them for who they are. If a Little Brother is having problems in life, a Big Brother should take the time to understand the situation but not overanalyze it. A Little Brother may occasionally act weird around his Big Brother. Rather than think he is a bad kid, a Big Brother must try to understand any troubling behavior. Perhaps there are issues at home, school, or with peers. A Big Brother should offer his support and willingness to listen but should not push. A Little Brother will talk when he is ready.

Use the Back Door

Direct attempts to build relationships with Little Brothers who do not trust adults can backfire. Simply telling them, "You can trust me," or "Don't worry, I'm your friend," might not work. But when a Big Brother meets some other less threatening need, the Little Brother will end up having an easier time connecting. Most boys, no matter how troubled, have a special interest that may be the key to the back door. A Big Brother should make an attempt to find that special interest and engage his Little Brother through it.

John Simon, a Big Brother with Big Brothers Big Sisters in Northeast Ohio, found a special interest with his second Little Brother, Sam, that helped him open up.

John and Sam, then 12 years old, were matched in March of 1989. A year prior to that, Sam's parents had divorced, leaving Sam both angry and very quiet.

While John wanted Sam to talk and voice his opinions and emotions, he knew he would have to find a comfortable way for him to do so. John knew that one of Sam's interests was video games. While John knew little about video games, he decided to go with Sam one day to a video arcade. John asked Sam to show him and teach him how to play Sam's favorite games. The normally untalkative Sam happily explained his favorite games and taught John how to play them. It was in this environment that Sam began to open up. From that day on, Sam knew he had a friend on his side. Today, Sam is studying to be a chef at the Culinary Institute in Pittsburgh. He was the best man at John's wedding where he proudly gave a five-minute speech.

When Big Brothers discover their Little Brothers' special interests, it is a good practice to pursue those interests. By doing so, a Big Brother helps create a comfortable environment that becomes a foundation for trust and openness. Sometimes the key to opening Little Brothers up to the gifts they have to share is found at the back door.

Show that You Care

Little Brothers who are wary of adult men will not assume that a Big Brother cares about them in the absence of some concrete evidence. While Little Brothers may not say so outright, their actions often indicate that they are seeking respect. They want to be noticed just like everyone else does. However, as Little Brothers get older, some Big Brothers are less comfortable expressing affection, particularly physically. Big Brothers can still nurture their Little Brothers by taking special note of them and their activities.

When talking with a Little Brother, a Big Brother should project a genuine interest in his Little Brother's daily life. Big Brothers, however, should avoid overanalyzing everything a Little Brother says. Giving time, whether it is in-person or even for ten minutes on the phone, is certainly the best proof of a Big Brother's concern. Little Brothers also take note of subtle symbols of special interest that Big Brothers show. Most positive interactions—such as humor, high-fives or other spontaneous gestures of friendliness—take only an instant of time. Sometimes just registering that a Big Brother has noticed some change in his life—a new haircut or how tall he is getting—gives a Little Brother a strong sense that his Big Brother cares about him.

Jim Formato, a 38-year-old Big Brother with Catholic Big Brothers in New York City, always takes the time to notice his Little Brother Michael, his match since 1991. "I always make sure that I'm very positive around him. I tell him he's a good-looking kid and always try to plug him with positive feedback. I make sure to tell him how much he's improved in sports like basketball."

For many Little Brothers, showing that a Big Brother cares is simply a matter of being there. Paul Dascoli, a former Little Brother in Rhode Island and two-time Big Brother, recalls the importance of dialogue with his Big Brother, Don Placido. "It was not important to me to go to a movie every week or go bowling or have him buy me anything. It was important to me for him to listen and ask about the week and sound enthusiastic about the same things that I was interested in doing. It was important that he was there to listen to me when I was having a problem and help me make the right choices."

In the 20 years that they have know each other, Don has always shown Paul that he cared. Whether it has been tracking his career progression, going to his out-of-state wedding, or simply giving friendly advice, Don has always been there. And what an interesting career progression it has been for Paul who has worked for Pepsi and Revlon, and last year became Vice President and Chief Financial Officer for Thomasville Furniture Industries in Thomasville, North Carolina.

Another great way to show that a Big Brother cares is to recognize special times in a Little Brother's life, such as birthdays, special holidays, match anniversaries, or graduations. I know it was important to Tony when I went to his eighth grade graduation. We took pictures, went out to lunch and even went to show off his diploma at the Big Brothers Big Sisters office.

Keep in mind that special times can have greater significance than just an important day. Big Brothers should take the time to notice events that may seem insignificant, like a good grade, a hit in a ballgame, or just trying something new. A Big Brother should not wait for a "big event" to show that he cares. Every Little Brother needs love, so do not be afraid to show it. That does not mean a Big Brother needs to push love either. It has to be genuine when both people in the match are ready for it.

Focus on Strengths

It is also important for a Big Brother to show his Little Brother that he likes him for who he is. Big Brothers must take the time to encourage their Little Brothers by accentuating their positive attributes. A Big Brother should tell his Little Brother what he likes about him and why. Men and boys need and crave respect. And since a man cannot affirm himself, Big and Little Brothers need to do it for each other.

Little Brothers grow best when they are supported and praised for their strengths. Little Brothers cannot build bridges around shortcomings until there is confidence in their own strengths. One way to focus on strengths is to choose activities in which the Little Brother can be successful. Nothing breeds confidence like success. New challenges can be met later when the relationship is stronger. With Tony, I realize that doing hands-on activities like drawing, model building, pumpkin carving, and puzzles help him complete projects that he can be proud of and display.

It is important for Big Brothers to communicate high expectations of Little Brothers. Big Brothers should not set unrealistic expectations, but they can let their Little Brothers know they believe in them and their capabilities. Doing this will go a long way toward helping Little Brothers overcome any negative self-images. Sometimes these negative self-images show up in activities that Little Brothers have never tried or experienced. Big Brothers often hear Little Brothers make comments like, "I could never do that." The best response a Big Brother can give is, "How do you know if you haven't tried?"

A Big Brother should always deal with his Little Brother on the assumption that the Little Brother would always like to put his best foot forward. No matter what their circumstances, all Little Brothers have positive qualities. Taking the time to let a Little Brother know his good traits and positive achievements will go a long way toward helping him begin to build bridges to success.

Be Sensitive to Differences and Value Them

Big and Little Brothers come from different backgrounds, neighborhoods, and upbringings. These differences may lead a Little Brother to react to his Big Brother in specific ways. In some cases Little Brothers may not want to acknowledge to their peers that they have a Big Brother, because it identifies that they do not have a dad, and therefore need a "substitute dad." Many Big Brothers address this issue up front by simply referring to their Little Brothers as their friends. There is nothing wrong with being proud of the program, but a Big Brother should be understanding of his Little Brother's position and what he might be thinking.

In other cases, like with Tony, having a Big Brother is viewed almost as a status symbol. Tony is proud to tell others what he did and where he went. He sees our relationship as something unique that other kids do not have.

Big Brothers should be sensitive to Little Brothers if they still have a father, because they may have very mixed feelings about their situations. No matter what their family circumstances, a Big Brother should never make his Little Brother feel bad about his situation or push him to talk about it unless he wants to do so. It is likely to be a very sensitive issue. If Little Brothers still have a father, Big Brothers should acknowledge that fact in some way because the father may still be symbolically important to the Little Brother.

Sometimes Little Brothers are not particularly proud of their neighborhoods or living situations. A Big Brother can help his Little Brother by simply doing the same thing over and over—showing him that he likes him for who he is. In time a Little Brother will sense that his Big Brother really is there for him, and that nothing would stand in the way of the match.

Set Limits

It is important for a Big Brother to let his Little Brother know what is important to him in the relationship. That means it is okay to set guidelines with a Little Brother. It is important to emphasize responsibility, accountability, and respect to a Little Brother. If a Big Brother is too permissive, he may be seen as a pushover and actually will have little influence on his Little Brother

A Big Brother should not hesitate to set reasonable limits on his Little Brother's behavior. A Big Brother should let his Little Brother know what he expects and why. A Little Brother may test a Big Brother's limits from time to time to see if he will stick around or just be another adult who abandons him. Little Brothers in general respond more positively when they begin to sense that their new Big Brother is in their lives as a friend rather than as another "know-all" adult, like a teacher or counselor with a preestablished agenda.

There are times when a Little Brother may be deceptive out of insecurity. A Big Brother should emphasize how important values like honesty and truthfulness are to him. As a Little Brother gains confidence in his Big Brother, his need to test will diminish.

A Big Brother should always make the time spent with his Little Brother meaningful. This symbolizes a respect and appreciation for each other. But if a Little Brother is testing the limits too often, a Big Brother should not hesitate to talk with his caseworker. It is essential that a Big Brother keeps his poise and never physically disciplines a Little Brother. A Big Brother has the opportunity to show a Little Brother how to handle himself simply by example.

Model Respect and Set a Good Example

A Big Brother should teach a Little Brother the importance of self-respect and respect for others. A Big Brother needs to remember to support his Little Brother even when his actions are not lovable—these are moments when a Little Brother most needs to hear words of encouragement. Even if a Little Brother's behavior is immature, a Big Brother must guard against treating his Little Brother as if he were a small child.

Tom Hammer, a former Little Brother and three-time Big Brother in Tulsa, Oklahoma, with Big Brothers Big Sisters of Green County, advises, "Don't try to come across as another adult trying to tell them what to do. With my Little Brothers, I am their friend. I'm not there to talk down to them or be their disciplinarian. They don't need that. I try to treat them with respect, and they in turn treat me with respect. I try to treat them as my equal. I think they appreciate my giving them that chance. I'm not their father. If I find out that one of them has done something, I don't turn around and call him and say 'What happened?' I might ask him how school is going and see if he'll talk about it. I don't want to make it seem that I'm on somebody else's side of things. He needs someone to understand and listen to his point of view. There may be things a Little Brother does that I don't agree with, but I need to respond not necessarily as a parent would, but maybe as a friend would."

A Big Brother should not give up on his Little Brother if at all possible. By sticking around when a Little Brother expects him to give up, the Big Brother sends a very powerful message. It tells a Little Brother that he is really worth something and that his Big Brother cares enough to be there.

Show a Little Brother All Sides of Being a Man

Little Brothers can benefit simply by seeing their Big Brothers as they are—men who have ups and downs in their lives just like everyone. That means a Big Brother should be open and honest about his feelings and experiences and share them with his Little Brother.

Some Big Brothers focus too hard on trying to be the perfect role model. As a result, they miss a valuable opportunity to teach their Little Brothers that every man has fears and concerns.

Jeff Venable, a Big Brother to Joseph since 1990, believes that, "It's important to show him times when I have self-doubt, or insecurity, or to admit when I'm wrong, as well as times when I'm confident. It's important to show all aspects of what it is to be a man, and not just put up a strong front attitude. I want him to see that men can be human beings with real problems and real feelings that they can express."

Showing a Little Brother all sides of being a man means being truthful with him and yourself. A Big Brother should not pretend he "knows it all" to impress his Little Brother. Little Brothers do not expect their Big Brothers to know everything. More than anything, Little Brothers appreciate honesty and sincerity.

Being honest and open also involves a Big Brother sharing some of his experiences growing up, both good and bad. I have talked with Tony about my father's death and about other issues I had growing up. By sharing my feelings with him, I feel that Tony knows me better, and in turn, he realizes that everyone has to deal with difficulty. Helping Little Brothers know that Big Brothers had growing pains too, some of which may have been similar to their own, builds a Little Brother's confidence that his Big Brother accepts him for who he is.

Keep Positive Expectations Alive

No matter what their circumstance, most Little Brothers have hopes and dreams. Big Brothers can help kindle the belief that great things can happen in their lives. That does not mean Big Brothers should plant unrealistic expectations or beliefs in Little Brothers' heads. But Big Brothers should find ways to channel their Little Brothers' enthusiasm. For example, if a Little Brother says he wants to become an actor or athlete (which we know is difficult), a Big Brother should use the opportunity to talk about the importance of education and careers. Give Little Brothers examples of people who have worked hard to achieve success and happiness.

I constantly tell Tony that he can be whatever he wants, and that the only person who can stand in his way is himself. I try to connect the things that he wants with what is necessary to get them. If he talks about the type of car he wants, we talk about how he can get it through working.

Derek Evans, a former Little Brother now living in Yellow Springs, Ohio, and a teacher of at-risk youth, recalls what his Big Brother, Ozzie Newsome, did for him. "Ozzie gave me a sense of hope, and I think hope is something a lot of people take for granted. A Big Brother gives a young boy hope that for the next hour, the next day, the next week, he can go on, it's not as bad as it seems, and it can be better. There are no guarantees, but you see you have more choices than you know. I think being a Little Brother saved my life, because it showed me that somebody out there did care."

Part of keeping positive expectations alive is making a Little Brother aware that he does have options in life. I try to emphasize to Tony that none of the events in his past, like his father dying when he was younger, can be changed. But I reinforce that he can influence what happens from this point on. I let him know that he does have a choice about the type of person he is and that he is in complete control of that choice. I do not try to downplay or expect Tony to forget anything in his past, but I do tell him that a person's past does not have to determine his future.

Keeping positive expectations alive for a Little Brother is an important building block to developing confidence and the resiliency to deal with challenges as they arise throughout life. When a Little Brother believes that many good things are still possible for him, it opens other doors of opportunity for him.

Be Patient

If there is one word that could serve as a criterion for being a successful Big Brother, it is "patience." A Little Brother will not immediately put all his faith in his Big Brother, because he must be certain that his Big Brother is really his friend. The development of trust takes time. Some Little Brothers are extremely shy, others are overbearing or even hostile at times to cover up their own insecurities. Such actions may be their way of testing their Big Brother's true interest in them. It is important to give a Little Brother opportunities to earn trust. One Big Brother I interviewed believes that trust is developed through a pattern of how the Big Brother acts. He says, "It was just consistency and dependability and honesty that allowed him to trust me. I treated him the same way I treated everyone else around me and he saw that and knew that I was sincere."

Eric Asch, a Big Brother in Scottsdale, Arizona, believes that communication and conversation help develop trust, but that, "It's not forced. Often the most important talks we have are an outgrowth of one of the activities we do." Under these conditions, his Little Brother, Brent, feels comfortable discussing issues that are on his mind. "And more often than not," Eric says, "it's not what I say but the way that I say it that stands out."

Building a relationship takes time. A Little Brother can test his Big Brother's limits, but a Big Brother needs to hang on and exercise patience. Sometimes Little Brothers can seem like they could not care less if their Big Brothers are there or not, but Little Brothers do care. They may not express it to their Big Brothers, but they do remember.

Give Seeds Time to Grow

All Big Brothers like to get instant feedback on how they are doing to determine if they are truly making an impact. The trouble is they often do not get this feedback. This leaves many Big Brothers frustrated and concerned that their efforts are not making a difference. Sometimes Big Brothers wonder if their Little Brothers are even listening to what they say or think their Little Brothers act as if what they say makes absolutely no sense.

Many Big Brothers make the mistake of overanalyzing every meeting they have and every move they make. They fret over missed opportunities and things they could have said or done differently. As a result, Big Brothers often place an unfair burden of perfection on themselves. It is key for Big Brothers to relax and realize that mistakes will be made and are to be expected. Big Brothers cannot expect change overnight, nor can they make decisions for their Little Brothers, no matter how much they may want to do so.

The reality is that a Big Brother may never fully know the impact of the time spent with a Little Brother. What we do know is that Little Brothers do listen and think about what their Big Brothers say, even though they do not always show it. I am constantly amazed at what Tony remembers from early on in our match almost six years ago. He remembers activities, places, and moments that I have forgotten.

Larry Wagner, an African-American bank executive in Cleveland, Ohio, who was a Big Buddy with Youth Visions, believes, "If you just focus on giving kids time and attention, they will end up doing well. Everyone has value until it gets tapped and tweaked. With a Little Brother, you plant the seed, and nurture it, and see it grow and bear fruit. You get to see a life change before you." For Larry, simply spending time with his Little Brother Mark has paid off. Mark is now married and has a good job with the City of Cleveland. Larry was the best man at Mark's wedding.

Whether Big Brothers are aware of it or not, every time they get together with their Little Brothers, they are in some way, contributing positively to their Little Brother's growth and development, as well as their own. A Big Brother may not see the impact, but it is there. As John Pearson, executive director of the Big Brothers Association of Greater Boston often has reminded me, "No time spent with a Little Brother is ever wasted."

The guidelines throughout this chapter offer an important reassurance to Big Brothers. Little Brothers report that what is most important to them is for their Big Brothers to *be there*, to *listen*, to *be honest*, and to *share experiences*.

Living the Impact

Letters from Little Brothers[3]

Big Brothers Big Sisters of Charlotte County, Florida

Big Brothers often become so discouraged in their relationships with their Little Brothers that they consider ending the match. They are discouraged because they wonder if they are making any impact at all.

It is important to remind Big Brothers that their efforts do make a difference. To ensure that their Big Brothers and Sisters understand the importance of their work, Big Brothers Big Sisters of Charlotte County holds an annual Appreciation dinner. Each year the Littles write brief letters about what their Bigs mean to them. When the letters are read and presented, "There are very few dry eyes in the room," says executive director Karen Fleury. "After the dinner, the Bigs realize the big impact they are making in the child's life, and the match is revitalized." These are some of the letters from the 1996 dinner.

What Is a Big Brother?

"A Big Brother is somebody that takes you places and cares for you. . . They also cheer you up when you're down. Basically he's your best friend.

"Thank you for being my Big Brother Joe."

David Vincent

"My Big Brother Bob is my friend, my mentor, and someone I look up to and know I can always turn to him if I ever need him. He teaches me many things like chess, hackey sack, and other games. He shows how to respect and care for the earth and all living beings. I hope someday I can be a Big Brother just like Bob."

Love,
Andy

"Dwayne is a very important person in my life. He guides me in the direction I need to be heading. When things are in turmoil Dwayne is there to put me right back on track. He is now showing me the joys of living independently. I show him how to win Scrabble with one word. I guess you could say that Dwayne is an all-around type of guy."

Sincerely,
Josh Leathers

"My name is Robbie and Ron is my Big Brother. He has been my best friend for 4 years and now we move into year number 5. Ron you are such a special person and I can't even think of what some of the things I would have gotten into if I didn't have you in my life. I wish I could have had a father like you. Ron I just want you to know you're my best friend. Even when I don't show it and sometimes it's a lot! I am glad we stuck it out buddy. It's great to know you will always be there."

Your friend,
Robbie

Why I Like My Big Brother

"I like my big brother because he is always there when I need him and when I need someone to talk to. I like being around him because he keeps me in line. But there's one thing I can say, 'I thank God for my Big Brother.'

"I wish that my friends have a Big Brother just like mine."

Yours truly,
Keith Bennett
("I'll always love my Big Brother")

"A Big is someone who really wants to make a difference in a young person's life. A Big is a person who has lots of things to share, such as love, caring, nurturing, and desire to help those less fortunate.

"Many Bigs have families of their own and are motivated by the opportunity to make a difference. A Big is not someone whose only interest is themselves, they go far beyond that. A Big becomes part of your immediate family, someone to talk with when things never seem to go right, someone who will listen and advise and give a hand when needed. They ask nothing in return but for you to be the best that you can. I hope someday, I, too, will become a Big for my Bigs have demonstrated to me that giving is certainly more rewarding than taking.

"I will always cherish the many special moments that they unselfishly gave to me. That is why I consider myself special to have wonderful Bigs that will always be there."

Love always,
Brett Wiggins

What Is a Big Brother?

B   Bold like superman

I   Intelligent

G   Good friend

B   Big-hearted

R   Rich in humor

O   Out-going

T   Thoughtful

H   Helpful

E   Entertaining

R   Really fun to be with

A Big Brother is Dan Wright.

From your Little Brother,
Philip James

Other Ways to Make a Big Impact

"Just because I can't do everything, doesn't mean I can't do something."

Martin Luther King

=◎= =◎= =◎=

Big Impact: Devin Rowling[1]

Big Brothers Big Sisters of Greater Des Moines, Iowa

Despite having three children of his own and a restaurant that keeps him busy 70 to 80 hours a week, Devin Rowling finds plenty of time to support Big Brothers Big Sisters of Greater Des Moines. He also has a very good reason to do so. Devin was a Little Brother back when he was in third grade in Cedar Falls, Iowa. His parents separated when he was two years old. His mother wanted Devin to have the support of an adult male friend since she was trying to put herself through school and had limited time to spend with him.

Some 25 years later in 1993, Devin opened his restaurant, the Cosi Cucina Italian Grill. The restaurant has received critical acclaim from Bon Appetit *and* Food & Wine *magazines, and is known as one of Des Moines' best restaurants despite little advertising. When Big Brothers Big Sisters was looking to do a fund-raiser, they approached Devin. His restaurant participated in what was known as "Calories for Kids," a fund-raiser where proceeds from weekend dessert sales are donated. The first year, Devin's restaurant came in second among donations. Refusing to be outdone, the next year Devin's restaurant was the largest contributor.*

Devin also has used his restaurant and its resources to educate people about Big Brothers Big Sisters of Greater Des Moines and its waiting list of more than 100 boys and girls. Every guest check has a small caption mentioning Big Brothers Big Sisters. Restaurant patrons are greeted by a painting of a boy and a man walking toward a ball field with the title, "Help make a difference. Be a Big Brother or Sister." The painting was commissioned by a friend of Devin's who owns a gallery. Devin also helps the agency spread the word by sponsoring radio, newspaper, and magazine advertisements.

This past August Devin joined the board of Big Brothers Big Sisters and firmly believes in their mission and the need in every community. "Kids get into trouble when they don't have good role models. They need to see a goal-oriented person. That's what this country is desperately lacking." Devin also believes that getting involved with Big Brothers Big Sisters is a two-way street. "It's just as rewarding for the Bigs as it is for the Littles. Many people complain about what is going on in society, but never do anything about it. If you ever want to make a difference, getting involved with Big Brothers Big Sisters is one way to do it. I think you get a lot more out of this world when you're doing good things for other people." Devin hopes to be a Big Brother himself one day when his children get older. For now, it is safe to say that Devin Rowling is doing all he can to have a Big Impact.

≥◎≤ ≥◎≤ ≥◎≤

Support Our Children

Not everyone is suited to be a Big Brother or Big Sister. Some people simply are not able to make the commitment or do not believe it is "their thing." But the responsibility of helping our children does not end there. Every Big Brothers Big Sisters agency requires support and involvement from the community. There are a number of ways that talents and skills can be used to make an impact in the life of a child, and all Big Brothers Big Sisters agencies have areas needing your help. More often than not, the ways you can help the most are simply by making use of the resources you already have.

This chapter looks at some of the areas where you can play a part. If you know that you want to help your local program in some way but are not sure how, the best advice I can give you is to call your local office and set up a time to talk and find out where your talents can best be utilized. Every successful team is made up of individuals who play different supporting roles. Every little bit helps collectively to make a big impact.

Enhance Recruiting Efforts

The tremendous need for Big Brothers puts volunteer recruitment at the top of every agency's list of needs. One way you can enhance the existing recruiting efforts of your local agency is by sharing Big Brothers Big Sisters program information with peers, business associates, and everyone you know. Challenge your friends, employees, neighbors, team members, and relatives to become a Big Brother or Big Sister. There is probably no greater compliment or tribute you could give someone than to say, "You know, I think you'd make a great Big Brother."

Many agencies have annual volunteer recruitment drives that aim to recruit a specific number of volunteers. These campaigns require a variety of resources to make them successful. Do you work for a company or belong to some organization or club that may have potential volunteers or sponsors? If so, see if that organization would hold an information session for Big Brothers Big Sisters. Volunteers are needed to organize on-site information sessions at their workplaces to recruit potential Big Brothers or to staff volunteer fairs and speak at these events on behalf of Big Brothers Big Sisters.

Several Big Brothers Big Sisters agencies have speakers bureaus of men and women who will speak on the agency's behalf. Some of the places that would be appropriate to hold speaking events include: corporations, service groups, military bases, retired groups, professional associations, volunteer groups, clubs and activities groups, fraternities, religious organizations, and ethnic groups. Help educate people about Big Brothers Big Sisters. Every opportunity to speak about our work makes an impact on the community.

Help with Fund-raising

All agencies are privately funded and therefore are entirely dependent upon the public for support every year. Agencies receive donations of all kinds, from direct support to in-kind services. Perhaps your company would sponsor or underwrite a fund-raising event. Agencies always need help with direct solicitation efforts and with coordinating special events and securing sponsorships for them. All events need volunteers to help run the events, notify the public, and gather donations of goods and services.

Agencies around the country hold different types of fund-raising events. Many have auctions, golf and sports tournaments, road races, and dinners, to name just a few. You can be part of a committee to help plan and promote an event, or share ideas for new events.

Bowl For Kid's Sake

One of the major fund-raising events each year that most agencies participate in is a national campaign called Bowl For Kid's Sake. Usually an agency's largest fund-raiser, Bowl For Kid's Sake is a bowl-a-thon in which participants get pledges to bowl.

This fun, lighthearted event involves individuals or teams signing up to bowl a game and collecting pledges or straight donations. You or your company can sponsor or join a Bowl For Kid's Sake team. Some companies form teams and challenge other companies to raise money. You can also be part of the group that helps plan the event at your Big Brothers Big Sisters agency. The fund-raiser is another great way to become directly involved with the program and meet the people who are making an impact.

Help Our Messages Reach the Public

Big Brothers Big Sisters agencies can never get enough positive public relations. There are a number of ways you can get involved to help ensure that our messages reach the public and the media. Some agencies publish a newsletter and are on the Internet. Others do neither. Many could use your help in developing a newsletter or a web page or some other marketing campaign. Many agencies need help developing publicity campaigns, while others need writers and photographers to cover events and write stories for use in newsletters, publications, and press releases. Some efforts can be as simple as writing a letter to your local paper in support of Big Brothers Big Sisters. If you have skills or know people who work in areas, such as photography, artwork, graphics, desktop publishing, writing, or printing, then Big Brothers Big Sisters can use your help. Use you creativity and come up with your own way of promoting Big Brothers Big Sisters.

Join an Advisory Board or Committee

All Big Brothers Big Sisters agencies have a board of directors. Many also have committees or groups that focus on specific tasks, such as a fund-raising event or a marketing campaign. Every board has a need for greater involvement from the community. Each agency has slightly different requirements to become a board or committee member, so check with them to see where you best fit.

Sponsor Events for Unmatched Boys

As mentioned before, some boys wait years to be matched. With the lengthy list of boys waiting to be matched at each agency, it is important to provide activities for them that remind them that we still care. Many agencies sponsor activities for waiting Littles. Big Brothers Big Sisters of Southern Nevada has developed its own SWAT team, which stands for Special Waiting Activities Team.

But for most waiting children, each day is a missed opportunity. If you or people you know have access to resources in the community, you may want to assist in planning an activity for waiting Littles. It does not have to be a big event. One man I interviewed takes waiting Littles out on his sailboat a couple of times a year. The kids love it and get to learn about sailing. Another man arranges through his parks and recreation department to have a field reserved once a summer to host a cookout and softball game, while another has a basketball court reserved once a month to sponsor pick-up basketball games. Helping plan activities for waiting Littles is a great way to show that you care and gives you an opportunity to meet some of the waiting children. And sometimes, getting other people you know interested in activities for waiting Littles encourages them to get more involved. Activity possibilities are endless, so check with your local agency.

Learn about Big Brother Councils

As mentioned, some agencies have councils of active Big Brothers and others interested in helping them. Each council usually works to bring matches together through projects and group activities, many of which include day trips, outings, and other volunteer projects. Even if you are not a Big Brother, you can help your local Big Brother Council plan or sponsor activities.

Start a Program or Affiliate in Your Area[2]

Despite the more than 500 Big Brothers Big Sisters agencies in the United States, many counties with single-parent households do not have a Big Brothers Big Sisters program. Big Brothers Big Sisters of America can help you learn all the requirements to start a program or an affiliate of an existing program in your area. While the process requires a lot of work and planning, many dedicated citizens have successfully started programs after learning that their communities were not being served by a Big Brothers Big Sisters program.

When Daryl Alderson was a Big Brother while at Arizona State more than 25 years ago, he never thought he'd ever lead such a group.

However, upon returning to his hometown of Joliet, Illinois, after graduation, Daryl found there was no Big Brothers Big Sisters agency serving his community. He took it upon himself to change that. Daryl helped set up a program while he was still working as a teacher in the Joliet school system. "I wanted to reach out to children who aren't involved in Little League, Girl Scouts, Boy Scouts, music lessons and other activities most people think are traditional youth activities," Alderson said. "A community raises children. I want Big Brothers Big Sisters to be their community." This year, Big Brothers Big Sisters of Will and Grundy Counties, with Alderson as its executive director, will mark 27 years of service to the community. They are also one of the largest agencies in the country, providing adult companionship and guidance for about 700 young people.

Help in the Office

Most agencies have little if any administrative staff, so they always need help with mailings, data input, and other office projects. This type of work is not glamorous, but it can be fun and is a great opportunity to learn more about the work that Big Brothers Big Sisters is doing. Even if you only have a couple of hours here and there, time spent helping a Big Brothers Big Sisters agency is never wasted. Helping staff coordinate administrative projects allows them to focus on meeting the most critical need—serving more children.

Everyone Can Do Something

You do not have to be a well-known society figure to make a big impact. As an individual or as part of a company, you can help children in a variety of ways. This can be as simple as talking with a friend, co-worker, or neighbor, or as big as starting a program in your area. Every bit of time and energy you can devote counts. By using the ideas, talents, and skills that you already have, you can directly contribute to the mission of Big Brothers Big Sisters. Contact your local Big Brothers Big Sisters agency, ask them how you can help, and offer your suggestions and input.

chapter

10

The Challenge

"...A lot of the problems facing our children are problems of

the human heart, problems that can only be solved when there

is a one-on-one connection, community by community, neigh-

borhood by neighbor, street by street, home by home, with

every child in the country entitled to live out their God-given

destiny."

President Bill Clinton
The Presidents' Summit on America's Future
April, 1997

$\geqq \textcircled{\tiny 6} \leqq$ $\geqq \textcircled{\tiny 6} \leqq$ $\geqq \textcircled{\tiny 6} \leqq$

Big Impact:
What Being Rich's Little Brother Means To Me

by Antone Merrill

I have been a Little Brother to Rich for about six years now, and in that time the bond between us has gotten stronger. I think I can tell Rich just about anything. I can always tell him something and ask him not to tell anyone else and I know he won't. The other side of having an older person in your life is that Rich has been through many of the problems I have, so that makes it easier to talk to him.

Our friendship is not just about talking. We also have lots of fun. We go to water parks, baseball games, camping, and other fun adventures. This past year we got to meet another match, Kenny Gordon and Phillip Henry. I remember how Phillip talked about how different his life would have been without Kenny. I know I feel the same way about Rich because there have been many times that I probably would have gotten in a lot of trouble if Rich was not around.

My favorite thing about having a Big Brother is having someone to talk to and do things with that I've never done before. As a Little Brother, I have learned about responsibility. Rich has really stuck with me through a lot. Having a Big Brother, you know someone will always be there for you and there will be lots of good times. To me, being a Little Brother is about a friendship that has been built and grown over the past six years.

It is important for kids that don't have a father or father figure to have someone older to help guide them and teach them to be stronger. Kids need role models. The Big Brothers program is a great program, and without it, I would have caused a lot of trouble. I have made a lot of choices I should not have made, but in the long run I have remained pretty straight.

With Rich, I have someone that can help me do things that I couldn't accomplish before. I want to go into the military one day and go to technical school after that to become a computer tech-

nician. Having a Big Brother, you know someone will always be there for you and there will be lots of good times. Knowing Rich means that I will always have someone I can turn to.

≥⊙≤ ≥⊙≤ ≥⊙≤

A Need for Caring Adults

The nuclear family of today, whatever its makeup, cannot in general, raise boys alone. Many boys no longer have the support network or contact with supportive, adult males in the community they so desperately need. Yet boys without a community-wide support system will still pursue worth and empowerment. Boys seek from the adult male world the love that says that their talents, strengths, hopes, and dreams are worthy. Boys desperately seek a role, a purpose in life, and without one, they will find one any way they can get it. Boys who have little or no positive sense of their place in the world will have lower self-confidence, less pride, and far less motivation to contribute to society.

Boston Globe columnist Ellen Goodman described it best when she said, "For all the reams of research and jargon, the current troubled state of children in America can be summed up pretty much in one sentence: There aren't enough caring adults in their lives. Most of the adults that children now see live inside a television set."[1]

When adults in a community do not make childraising a primary focus, children feel unsafe and unloved. Boys in particular turn to other means of support and validation. Boys living without a life-defining or confident sense of spiritual purpose often become violent criminals, gang members, and sexual predators. Other boys become men unable to commit to long-term relationships with mates or unprepared to raise healthy children to adulthood.

While none of this is news to us, we are almost paralyzed by its daily impact. We become numb when we see another boy lost to the effects of violence, crime, sex, drug, and alcohol abuse. Most of us feel overwhelmed and helpless. How can we change the world when every day seems like it is worse and worse? How can we possibly affect the lives of so many? The answer is, more often than not—we cannot. We're too busy working, trying to keep up with our own lives. So we let ourselves off the hook. We're doing so much as it is, we say. How can we possibly do anything more?

Whether we acknowledge it or not, we are all paying the price for this attitude. The costs to society of boys who drop out of school, commit crimes, or produce children of their own are enormous. Yet, as criminality has moved to the top of local and national agendas, those on the front lines of youth crime say all the talk has not generated enough activism. Despite the urging of politicians, religious leaders, and even young people themselves, the volunteers needed to spend time with children are simply not turning out. Those who seem to speak loudest against violence and who demand action rarely devote time to the young people most at risk of committing crime or falling prey to it.

No one is immune to what is happening to our nation's boys. Yet while the search for the "cure" for the boys who have fallen through the cracks continues, there is a generation of boys standing at the crossroads. These are the boys who are highly vulnerable to the negative influences of society, but they are also the ones who are potentially still open to all the good the world has to offer. Time and time again we hear stories of boys who have beaten the odds despite their circumstances. More often than not, those stories involve relationships with supportive adult men. This leads us to believe that one of the best ways to reach boys is to provide them with one-on-one relationships with caring, mature adult men.

It Takes a Village

The often-used African proverb, "It takes a village to raise a child," recently immortalized in a book by First Lady Hillary Rodham Clinton, is as relevant today as ever. Children need a variety of resources from the community to develop into healthy, well-adjusted adults. Relationships with adult men can help boys without fathers understand and make sense of who they are. Men can also teach boys to respect themselves and others. Boys need men they can identify with positively and model themselves after.

Such relationships are not luxuries; they are essential. Boys from single-parent families often have little or no contact with supportive adult men in the community. Many boys do not even experience one significant relationship with an adult male outside their immediate family. Without a strong support network of men, boys are more likely to commit crimes, join gangs, drop out of school, get girls pregnant, and abuse drugs and alcohol. The choice we have as a society is clear—we can help shape our boys' futures or wait to let them shape us. Our challenge is to actively be part of creating that future, rather than passively watching the results of our inaction.

Volunteering as a Big Brother is just one way to contribute to the creation of a strong support network for boys. But as Marc Freedman points out, "Rather than thinking of mentoring as a sufficient solution to the problems of youths, we would do well to think of the mentoring movement as a potentially important step in the right direction—one that highlights an unmet need, goes part of the way toward addressing it, and calls out for reinforcement."[2] A Big Brother alone cannot change a boy's circumstances, nor is he ever asked to do so. But we know from research that boys who do have Big Brothers fare far better than boys who do not. It should not take a social scientist, however, to convince us that any child is better off when they have at least one relationship with an adult who provides unconditional, supportive friendship. The results of that friendship may not always be measured by numbers. We only hope that we can help boys grow into healthy, productive, well-adjusted adults.

It takes commitment and time to be a Big Brother. But it is more than just a commitment to a boy—it is a commitment to the community, to the future, and to the person who volunteers. Volunteering does not take as much time as you might think. Most Big Brothers do not look at it as an extra three or fours a week, they successfully find ways to incorporate their Little Brothers into activities they already do.

It does not take special skills to be a Big Brother. It does not require a person to have a lot of money, a big house, or a nice car. In general, any man who cares about children, enjoys working with them, knows how to listen and share experiences, is open, honest, consistent, and knows how to have fun, would make an excellent Big Brother.

In return for making a difference in the life of a boy, a Big Brother receives back some of the greatest gifts that money could never buy. Spending time with a Little Brother helps men relive many of the joys of childhood, while sharing new experiences. A Big Brother teaches his Little Brother many skills, and a Little Brother provides firsthand knowledge of what it means to be a boy growing up in America today.

My Challenge to the Men of America

If America is ever going to straighten itself out, the answers must start right in our own communities. April 1997 marked the first

Volunteerism Summit. President Clinton reminded America that, "Much of the work of America cannot be done by government alone. Government programs cannot solve the problems facing fatherless boys, and neither can the schools. Single-parent families need support from the community."

Whether men realize it or not, their presence matters to boys. Their contribution to boys is to listen, be understanding, and compassionate. To the extent that men connect with boys at a personal level and focus on their strengths, a man helps prepare a boy for a healthier, more productive adulthood.

Make a Difference to One

There is an old tale that goes something like this:

As the old man walked down a Spanish beach at dawn, he saw ahead of him what he thought to be a dancer. A young man was running across the sand, rhythmically bending down to pick up a stranded starfish and throw it far into the sea. The old man gazed in wonder as the young soul again and again threw the small starfish from the sand to the water. The old man approached and asked why the young man spent so much energy doing what seemed a waste of time. The young man explained that the stranded starfish would die if left until the morning sun.

"But there must be thousands of miles of beach and millions of starfish. How can your effort make any difference?" The young man looked down at the small starfish in his hand and, as he threw it safely into the sea, he said, "It makes a difference to this one."

The problems that face us will not go away overnight. At times, this fact appears so daunting that we feel like no effort could make any difference. But if we are ever to make a big impact, it must start as an effort by each individual—people helping people, one person at a time.

I challenge each upstanding, responsible man to become a Big Brother or to get involved with their local Big Brothers Big Sisters agency. Every man can do something to support this organization that has, for more than 90 years, been helping create and rewrite history. We need men of all ages, races, education levels, and professions to come forward to be Big Brothers and to make a big impact.

To find out more information about your local Big Brothers Big

Sisters program, check your local phone directory or contact:

Big Brothers Big Sisters of America National Office
230 North 13th Street
Philadelphia, PA 19107-1538

Phone: (215) 567-7000
Fax: (215) 567-0394
E-mail: bbbsa@aol.com
Web: http://www.bbbsa.org

To meet volunteers, agency staff, and other Big Brothers Big Sisters supporters from around the globe who share information and their experiences about Big Brothers Big Sisters, please join our E-mail discussion group. The list is run by Jerome Scriptunas, president of the board of Big Brothers Big Sisters of Monmouth County, New Jersey. Send an E-mail to Jerome at:

jeromes@worldnet.att.net

Appendix I

The State of Our Nation's Boys

According to the Children's Defense Fund, every day in America 6 youths under 20 commit suicide, 255 children under 18 are arrested for drug offenses, 318 are arrested for alcohol-related offenses, 327 are arrested for violent crimes, 2,217 students drop out of high school, and 5,504 children and youths under 18 are arrested for a variety of reasons.

Although the rate of juvenile violent crime arrests remained constant between 1973 and 1988, it increased by more than 50 percent between 1988 and 1992. The FBI reports that in 1992 there were an estimated 2.3 million juvenile arrests—nearly 130,000 for violent crimes. In 1994 alone, arrests for youths under age 18 for violent crimes surged by 7 percent. The number of youths under 18 arrested for murder rose 158.3 percent from 1985 through 1994.[1] The growth in homicides involving juvenile offenders has surpassed that of adult offenders.

James Alan Fox, dean of the Northeastern University college of criminal justice in Boston, calls this "the calm before the crime storm." An impending crime wave of teen violence is facing us as the adolescent population begins to rise in America. There are currently 39 million children under age 10, more than we have had for decades. The Juvenile Justice Clearinghouse Report indicates that by the year 2010, the juvenile population aged 10 to 17 is projected to grow by more than 20 percent over the 1990 Census. If juvenile arrest rates for Violent Crime Index offenses (murder, rape, robbery, and aggravated assault) were to remain fixed at the 1992 level, juvenile population growth alone would produce a 22 percent rise in violent crime arrests. However, should the juvenile violent crime arrest rates increase at the rate they have between 1983 and 1992, the number of arrests for these violent crimes would double by the year 2010 to more than 260,000 arrests.[2]

Today, more adolescents are using illicit drugs and the long-term impact is even more consequential. The 1995 Monitoring the Future study reports that if the estimated 39 million Americans under the age of 10 continues to abuse drugs at the same rate as today's youth, drug use will increase by alarming proportions. By the year 2000, 1.4 million high school seniors will be using illicit drugs monthly.[3]

While not all young people who use drugs drop out of high school, those who do drop out have a much higher rate of drug use than those who stay in school and graduate. The lifetime costs to an individual dropping out of high school are extremely high. Lost wages and benefits range from $563,000 to $900,000 per person. Those dropouts who become career criminals and heavy drug users cost taxpayers $1.9 to $2.7 million dollars per person during their lifetimes.[4]

Nearly 91 percent of violent crime is committed by males—most by young males. Between 1985 and 1992, the rate at which males ages 14 to 17 committed murder increased by about 50 percent for whites and more than 300 percent for blacks.

The future looks just as bleak. By 2005, the number of males in the 14 to 17 age group will have risen by about 25 percent. Many experts warn that the additional 500,000 boys who will be 14 to 17 years old in the year 2000 will mean at least 30,000 more murderers, rapists, and muggers on the streets than we have today[5].

Boys without fathers are especially at risk. They are less likely to finish high school, more likely to suffer emotionally and economically, and more likely to have difficulty forming relationships. Boys raised in fatherless homes with multiple problems often commit crimes that bring them into the juvenile court system, and carry inadequate parenting into the next generation. While many boys achieve great success and give all the credit to their strong, often single mothers, there are a lot of boys whose mothers, try as they might, cannot overcome the influence of the streets, gangs, and peer pressure.

Adolescent boys commit violent acts that get them in trouble with the law 50 times more than girls do. They are also two to three times as likely to get in trouble with the police, especially in neighborhoods with a high concentration of single-parent families.[6] On average, boys raised in single-parent homes show more aggressive and antisocial behavior than do boys in two-parent families.

As David Blankenhorn points out in his book, *Fatherless America,* "For most of our history, a child growing up in America could reasonably expect to grow up with a father at home. Today, he can reasonably expect not to."[7] The share of children living in mother-only families has increased from 6 percent in 1950 to 24 percent in 1994. For about

19 million children, life did not include a father in 1994. The fatherless phenomenon is so widespread that many children grow up in neighborhoods where it is unusual to spot a father living in a home. According to the Annie E. Casey Foundation, a Maryland-based charitable organization dedicated to helping build better futures for disadvantaged children in the United States, about 4.5 million children are living in areas where single-mother families comprise more than half of all families.[8] The National Fatherhood Initiative predicts that between 55 to 60 percent of children born in the 1990s will spend part of their childhood in a fatherless home.[9]

Statistics reflecting the effects of fatherless homes are alarming. Children from fatherless homes comprise 63 percent of youth suicides,[10] 90 percent of runaway and homeless children, 71 percent of high school dropouts,[11] 72 percent of adolescent murderers,[12] 60 percent of America's rapists,[13] 85 percent of children with behavioral disorders,[14] 75 percent of adolescents in chemical abuse centers,[15] and 70 percent of imprisoned minors.[16]

It has been conventional to argue that these kids would have a better chance if only the economics of single-parent families were better. It has also been argued that these children would be better off if they had a two-parent family. However, it would be an oversimplification to say that every boy would succeed if he only had two parents. Not all fathers are willing or able to make a positive contribution to family life. And there are many courageous and loving single parents who are able to balance the competing demands on their time and attention to care and provide for their children alone.

A major issue is simply time itself. Today's parents spend roughly 40 percent less time with their children than did parents a generation ago.[17] Almost 20 percent of sixth through twelfth graders have not had a good conversation lasting at least ten minutes with one of their parents in more than a month.[18] As psychologist Robert Coles sums up, "Parents are too busy spending their most precious capital—their time and energy—struggling to keep up with credit card payments. They work long hours, and when they get home at the end of the day, they're tired. And the kids are left with a Nintendo® or a pair of sneakers."[19] Today 1.6 million children age 5 to 14 return from school every day to a home devoid of adults.[20]

Appendix II

The Success of Big Brothers Big Sisters Agencies

Society is desperate for solutions to the problems that plague our youth. We want programs that will have a lasting impact that are not a burden on taxpayers. We also enjoy hearing about people who have overcome backgrounds fraught with despair, deprivation, and encounters with delinquency, to become distinguished, well-known adults.

With Big Brothers Big Sisters in existence for more than 90 years, one would expect dramatic stories of rags-to-riches, life-changing experiences. For sure, there are thousands of such cases. However, it is important to keep in mind that the primary objective of one-to-one friendship is simply to help children develop into normal, happy, well-adjusted adults. A Big Brother's focus is not to turn his Little Brother into a movie star or a brain surgeon, but to help him become a respected member of his community.

With that said, it is no longer sufficient to merely state that Big Brothers Big Sisters does good work. As all nonprofit organizations compete for shrinking dollars, they are required to prove to society and its funding sources the effectiveness of their work. Is the Big Brothers Big Sisters program making a difference in the lives of our youth? The answer, time and time again, is a resounding yes.

What the Research Shows[1]

Public/Private Ventures (P/PV), a research and development organization focusing on helping young people, conducted a comparative study of 959 10- to 16-year-olds who applied to eight accredited Big Brothers Big Sisters programs in 1992 and 1993. The participating Big Brothers Big Sisters agencies were in Philadelphia, Phoenix, Wichita, Minneapolis, Rochester, Columbus, Houston, and San Antonio. Half of these youths was randomly assigned to a treatment group, for which Big Brothers Big Sisters matches were made or attempted; the other half was assigned to waiting lists. P/PV compared the two groups after reaching teenagers, this program suggests a strategy the country can build on to make a difference, especially for youth in single-parent families," said Gary Walker, president of Public/Private Ventures.[2]

What stands out about these results is that they speak to a much different approach to youth policy. In contrast to the traditional problem-oriented approach, the study results were achieved simply by an adult providing nothing more than a caring, supporting friendship. The Big Brothers Big Sisters approach does not specifically target aspects of life like drug use or poor grades. "A positive youth development approach at this vulnerable age is likely to have more lasting results than programs focused on a specific behavior," said Thomas McKenna, national executive director of Big Brothers Big Sisters of America. Joseph P. Tierney, a PPV senior research associate and one of the three researchers on the projects, believes that, "It's important to have a friend, a buddy, to be there for them, to be a sounding board, to be nonjudgmental, to sit there and listen and understand what the kids are going through."

The program works because volunteers focus on meeting the "universal needs of young humans for consistent, supportive attention from an adult friend who cares."

Through studies, PPV has established that there is a commonality of five components in the lives of kids in at-risk situations who make it. They are: one caring adult; experiences that teach the value of work; extracurricular programs; opportunities to make good decisions; and support during transitions. Big Brothers Big Sisters services encompass all of these components.

One of the agencies in the study, Valley Big Brothers Big Sisters in Phoenix, Arizona, has had tremendous success with their program. The Little Brothers and Little Sisters in the program as compared to children in their county have:

- *a teenage pregnancy rate of 1 percent vs. 10 percent*
- *a 2 percent school dropout rate vs. 14 percent*
- *a rate of 12 per 1,000 of referrals to a juvenile detention center vs. 22 per 1,000*
- *a teen suicide rate of 0 percent vs. 16 per 100,000*

Several Big Brothers Big Sisters agencies, in addition to the ones who participated in the PPV study, regularly conduct their own program evaluations.

Big Brothers Big Sisters of Greater Manchester,
New Hampshire[3]

In the spring of 1994, Big Brothers Big Sisters of Greater Manchester conducted an evaluation of its program that involved 97 current and former Little Brothers and Little Sisters. The focus of the evaluation was on areas that reflect evidence in Littles of positive self-concept and goal-directed thinking. The areas included: educational achievement and goals; avoidance of substance abuse; delinquency; teenage parenting; career goals; and involvement in community activities.

The respondents of the survey, 49 males and 48 females, were asked to rate five statements on a scale of 1 to 10, with 10 being "strongly agree." In the first statement, "Having a Big was one of the best things that ever happened to me," 78 percent of the Littles responded with an "8" or better, with nearly 57 percent rating a "10." The statement "Having a Big has helped me to make smarter choices in my life," brought ratings of "8" or above from 72 percent of surveyed Littles. Another statement, "I felt comfortable talking to my Big about my feelings," drew a response of "8" or better for 74 percent of Littles. A fourth statement, "I did a lot of things I would not have been able to do," brought a response of 8 or better by more than 82 percent. Finally, the statement "Since having a Big, I find it easier to talk with adults," received rating of "8" or above from 57 percent of respondents.

Positive results were reported in academic achievement and educational goal setting as well. Seventy-nine of 97 respondents were currently enrolled in school, 11 had graduated and 1 had achieved a GED. Only 6 had dropped out of school, representing a 7 percent dropout rate. This compares very favorably with the 27 percent dropout rate reported in Manchester.

Findings were also favorable regarding drug and alcohol abuse. While the New Hampshire Office of Alcohol and Drug Abuse Prevention estimates that 20 percent of youth ages 12 to 19 are alcohol or drug abusers, the survey found only 7 percent indicating any use of illegal drugs "within the last 30 days."

Most respondents, 77 percent, reported never being in trouble with the law, and teen parenting did not seem to be a major problem. Only three respondents reported having one child each. Finally, almost 93 percent of respondents indicated an interest in becoming a Big Brother or Big Sister in the future. Overall, the survey suggests that the majority of youths served by the program have remained free from serious drug and alcohol abuse, legal problems, teen parenting, and premature discontinuation of schooling.

Big Brothers Big Sisters of Greater Manchester, New Hampshire[3]

In the spring of 1994, Big Brothers Big Sisters of Greater Manchester conducted an evaluation of its program that involved 97 current and former Little Brothers and Little Sisters. The focus of the evaluation was on areas that reflect evidence in Littles of positive self-concept and goal-directed thinking. The areas included: educational achievement and goals; avoidance of substance abuse; delinquency; teenage parenting; career goals; and involvement in community activities.

The respondents of the survey, 49 males and 48 females, were asked to rate five statements on a scale of 1 to 10, with 10 being "strongly agree." In the first statement, "Having a Big was one of the best things that ever happened to me," 78 percent of the Littles responded with an "8" or better, with nearly 57 percent rating a "10." The statement "Having a Big has helped me to make smarter choices in my life," brought ratings of "8" or above from 72 percent of surveyed Littles. Another statement, "I felt comfortable talking to my Big about my feelings," drew a response of "8" or better for 74 percent of Littles. A fourth statement, "I did a lot of things I would not have been able to do," brought a response of 8 or better by more than 82 percent. Finally, the statement "Since having a Big, I find it easier to talk with adults," received rating of "8" or above from 57 percent of respondents.

Positive results were reported in academic achievement and educational goal setting as well. Seventy-nine of 97 respondents were currently enrolled in school, 11 had graduated and 1 had achieved a GED. Only 6 had dropped out of school, representing a 7 percent dropout rate. This compares very favorably with the 27 percent dropout rate reported in Manchester.

Findings were also favorable regarding drug and alcohol abuse. While the New Hampshire Office of Alcohol and Drug Abuse Prevention estimates that 20 percent of youth ages 12 to 19 are alcohol or drug abusers, the survey found only 7 percent indicating any use of illegal drugs "within the last 30 days."

Most respondents, 77 percent, reported never being in trouble with the law, and teen parenting did not seem to be a major problem. Only three respondents reported having one child each. Finally, almost 93 percent of respondents indicated an interest in becoming a Big Brother or Big Sister in the future. Overall, the survey suggests that the majority of youths served by the program have remained free from serious drug and alcohol abuse, legal problems, teen parenting, and premature discontinuation of schooling.

Chattanooga, Tennessee Big Brothers Big Sisters

Chattanooga Big Brothers Big Sisters in Tennessee conducted a survey in 1992 and found that their Little Brothers and Little Sisters fared very well against state and national averages in the following categories:

	Chattanooga BB/BS	State	National
School Dropout Rate	4%	20%	10%
Alcohol Use Rate	3%	50%	20%
Teenage Pregnancy Rate	1%	10%	12%
College/Voc. School Rate	63%	32%	41%

Big Brothers Big Sisters of Santa Clara County, California

According to Big Brothers Big Sisters of Santa Clara County, "99 percent of our children who currently have a Big Brother or Big Sister are in school and plan to graduate, and 98 percent have never had a brush with the law."

Big Brothers Big Sisters of Northern Colorado

In 1995, out of 826 boys and 517 girls who had a Big Brother or Big Sister, 99.8 percent did not drop out of school, 98 percent had not experienced drug or alcohol problems, 98 percent of boys were not involved with gang activity, 93 percent were not adjudicated in juvenile court and 100 percent did not commit suicide.

Nutmeg Big Brothers Big Sisters, Connecticut [4]

In Hartford, Nutmeg Big Brothers Big Sisters case managers evaluated the success of their matches and found that: 77 percent of the children achieved an improvement in school grades; 63 percent improved their school behavior; 92.5 percent stayed free of alcohol and illegal drugs; and 96 percent stayed away from gangs. This in an area where in Hartford, 18 percent of all public school students drop out, and in Connecticut, 23 percent of eighth graders had an alcoholic drink within the past 30 days.

The results of these programs all put an emphasis on prevention as the key to success.

Appendix III

Suggested Activities to Share with a Little Brother

1. Surprise your Little by celebrating his/her half birthday.

2. Make a thin layer of Jell-O and carve it into letters, numbers, figures, etc.

3. Together, write a family newspaper for friends and relatives.

4. Take a walk together with a memento bag and collect interesting leaves, rocks, or junk.

5. Go to the bank and open a savings account for him or her.

6. Design a Christmas/holiday card together.

7. Make a bug cage and catch bugs together.

8. Eat lunch with him/her at school.

9. Teach him/her to weave a ring out of grass.

10. Paint graffiti on the walls of a room a few days before it is repainted.

11. Buy ten shares of stock in an inexpensive company that he/she will recognize and watch it make or lose money.

12. Look up new words in a dictionary.

13. Use a globe to locate friends, travel destinations, and current events together.

14. Go on a sound scavenger hunt with a tape recorder.

15. Go shopping at a secondhand store for dress-up clothes.

16. Work together to make a collage of his/her life with pictures cut from magazines.

17. Make giant soap bubbles.

18. Plan a vacation together—imaginary or real.

19. Roast marshmallows with toothpicks over the flame of a candle.

20. Learn a simple magic trick to amaze him/her and friends.

21. Show him/her your picture from your high school yearbook.

22. Paint an original T-shirt for a special occasion.

23. Go for a walk through a hardware store and explain the function of various tools.

24. Compliment your Little's character and skill three times for every one compliment on his/her appearance.

25. On a one-foot square of grass, find all the living things that are visible in that space.

26. On his/her birthday, ask your Little to lie on butcher paper and trace around him/her. Repeat the process each year to show how much he/she has grown.

27. Learn to count to ten in a foreign language.

28. Take your Little to a volleyball or basketball game at the high school he/she will attend.

29. Write a letter to your Little on your anniversary telling what you've noticed about him/her in the past year.

30. Have an art show of his/her masterpieces. Invite your friends and relatives to come and buy original, signed artwork. Set low prices so everything will sell.

31. Practice filling out applications for everything.

32. Help your Little make homemade potpourri with dried flower petals.

33. Help your Little make a list of all the people who love him/her.

34. Look through a clothing catalog and ask what he/she likes and doesn't like. Explain what is becoming of a young lady/gentleman and what is not.

35. Wash the car together.

36. Explore the attic together.

37. Paint a special message for his/her mother on a wooden cutting board.

38. Make a calendar of the big events of his/her year.

39. Make snow angels.

40. Write a poem about him/her and read it on a special occasion.

41. Feed the birds.

42. Look through a book of house plans and help him/her pick out a dream home.

43. Help her write a letter to the author of a book she really likes.

44. Buy her a rubber stamp or stickers with his/her name and address on them.

45. Start a coin or stamp collection.

46. Get a book of animal tracks and explore a pond or trail together to see what animals live in the area.

47. Put colored water in a two-liter bottle. Connect another to it like an hourglass and turn it over. Give it a swirl and you will create a tornado in a bottle.

48. Go on a camera scavenger hunt together. Make a list of things you want pictures of before the hunt. Let him/her take the pictures.

49. Teach him/her a big word.

50. Tape record messages to send to grandparents or other loved ones who do not live nearby.

51. Help him/her stencil a border patter around the top of a wall.

52. Go on a newspaper scavenger hunt. Give him/her a list of 10 to 20 items to find in a newspaper.

53. Read biographies of people who did great things and let your Little know they were no different from him/her.

54. Make a weather board. Put a few hooks on a small board. Prepare tags with numbers and a few key words. Show him/her how track temperature and weather conditions each morning before school.

55. Learn to program a computer in BASIC language.

56. Finger-paint with chocolate, lemon, or strawberry pudding.

57. Make mini-pizzas using English muffins topped with pizza sauce, cheese, and pepperoni.

58. Make maracas by covering light bulbs with layers of paper-mache. When they dry, gently break the glass and paint them.

59. Help compose a letter to your Little's Congressional representative regarding an issue of importance to your Little.

60. Invite him/her to sell old toys and clothes at your garage sale.

61. Check out a tree identification book from the library and discover which ones are in your neighborhood.

62. Using the letters from a long word, see how many smaller words you can create.

63. Train together and participate in a 1K fun run.

64. Role play meeting new people so he/she will have more confidence in unfamiliar situations.

65. Invite someone who has lived in a foreign country over for dinner to talk about life in that country.

66. Use a book of names to find the meaning of his/her name and those of family members and friends.

67. Build a log cabin together with Popsicle sticks and glue.

68. Clip coupons together. Give him/her a percentage of what you save.

69. Watch a potter throwing on a wheel.

70. Use a magnifying glass together to examine all kinds of little things.

71. Make a tent using blankets stretched over chairs and tucked into drawers.

72. Teach him/her to use a fire extinguisher.

73. Squeeze fresh orange juice.

74. Tape record him/her reading a favorite story.

75. Tour the state capitol.

76. Go to the airport for lunch and watch the planes take off and land.

77. Show him/her photographs or movies of you as a child.

78. Roast pumpkin seeds in the oven.

79. Take him/her with you when you vote and explain why you selected the candidates you did.

80. Volunteer together to ring a bell for charity at Christmas time.

81. Ask him/her to share an opinion on things that are important to you.

82. Get some lumber, hammer, and nails, and encourage your Little to be creative.

83. Tell him/her stories about you when you were his/her age.

84. Volunteer to visit his/her class to tell students about your profession.

85. Teach him/her how to make a football spiral.

86. Have a sock war — five minutes and 20 pairs of socks.

87. Open the hood of a car and point out various parts of the engine.

88. Walk through an unfinished house.

89. Give him/her your old billfold or purse. "Accidentally" leave a dollar or two hidden inside.

90. Speak highly of the men and women in your life. Help him/her to value their character and skill.

91. Read books about famous inventors.

92. Enjoy a fresh coconut or pineapple together.

93. Watch the activity at a construction site.

94. Build and paint a birdhouse.

95. Teach your Little to tap out his/her name in Morse code or spell it using sign language.

96. Order sea monkeys or Chia pets and watch them grow.

97. Skip rocks on water.

98. Copy each other's hands on a photocopy machine.

99. Buy a yo-yo and learn how to do tricks with it.

100. Help him/her make a video movie.

101. Have business cards printed with his/her name and a catchy slogan.

102. Take him/her to a photo darkroom and see how negatives and prints are made.

103. Visit a farm and milk a cow.

104. Look in phone books to find the name of someone with the same name as you and your Little.

105. Visit the state legislature when it is in session.

106. Set up a roadside lemonade stand or similar business.

107. Teach him/her the proper way to answer the phone.

108. Using play money, show him/her how you spend the money you earn.

109. Make a list of everything you will do with all the money you win from the $10 million sweepstakes.

110. Get a chemistry set and perform your own experiments.

111. Encourage him/her to admire professional athletes who are worthy of his/her admiration on and off the field.

112. Write to the President and ask him for a photo. Your Little will receive a picture and a packet of information.

113. Have notepads imprinted with your Little's name.

114. Build a house of cards together.

115. Buy a short section of rain gutter and build a giant banana split in it together. Invite some friends to share the treat with you.

116. Make your own code with numbers representing letters. Send each other coded messages.

117. Teach your pet a new trick.

118. Visit a music store and learn about different types of instruments.

119. Visit a college.

120. Make pancakes from scratch.

121. Learn to identify three constellations.

122. Learn CPR together.

123. Teach him/her how to operate a washing machine and to sort or fold clothing.

124. Paint an old piece of furniture.

125. Learn ten new words in a foreign language.

126. Do something together for an elderly friend.

127. Rent a bicycle built for two and tour the arboretum.

128. Teach your Little a clean joke he can share with his/her friends and teachers.

129. Learn to use a real camera—one in which nothing is automatic.

130. Shop until you drop.

131. Go ice fishing or ice skating. Then, stop somewhere for hot chocolate when you're through.

132. Explore a Children's Museum.

133. Go to an airplane or military air show.

134. Go tubing or sledding down hill. Ask your Little to go first to "test it out."

135. Make dinner for your Little's mom and surprise her on her birthday.

136. Have a Monopoly tournament. Try to let your Little buy Park Place and Boardwalk.

137. Visit a hospital and look at the babies in the nursery or infant intensive care unit.

138. Shop for antiques in a rural community.

139. Surf the Internet. Try to tap into a computer in a foreign country. Or look for web pages of companies he/she would recognize.

140. Learn how to fix your bikes.

141. Visit a secondhand store and buy some old clothes that you can use to play "dress-up."

142. Go on a scavenger hunt through the Arboretum looking for as many signs of life or death as you can.

143. Visit a nursing home and read or sing to the residents. Or, ask them to describe what life was like when they were your Little's age.

144. Whack golf balls at the driving range.

145. Shop for hats bearing the insignia of your Little's favorite sports teams.

146. Walk around a boat show, sporting show, or Star Trek convention.

147. Bake and frost cutout cookies.

148. Rent a canoe and explore the lagoons in the Arboretum.

149. Assemble a model or bookcase.

150. Work on home improvement projects together—painting, wallpapering or remodeling a spare room. It provides great talk time and quite a few laughs, too.

151. Make foods from around the world and learn how people live in that country.

152. Have a carpet picnic on the living room floor and watch a movie.

153. Check out programs for kids on weekends at your local civic center.

154. Throw snowballs at phone poles from increasing distances.

155. Meditate together.

156. Take him/her to your place of worship.

157. Maintain a scrapbook of all the things you do together. Include ticket stubs, menus, pictures, brochures, programs, and other mementos.

158. Rearrange the furniture in your living room.

159. Visit a coffee shop to sip hot chocolate or soda while playing chess, checkers, or backgammon.

160. Munch pizza and play games at your local arcade parlor.

161. Research an important event or issue at the library. Tour the big libraries at the university.

162. Sit at the mall or in a park and watch people.

163. Sniff the flowers at your local Arboretum or garden.

164. Go apartment or house hunting.

165. Create s'mores with graham crackers, marshmallows, and chocolate chunks. Heat them in the oven, microwave, or over an open fire.

166. Learn how to dance.

167. Take turns styling each other's hair.

168. Learn to sew an outfit for your Little.

169. Do aerobics in the living room or visit a health center.

170. Decorate eggs— not just at Easter.

171. Visit someone whose yard you raked during the fall.

172. Make a homemade pizza.

173. Plan a trip around the world or around the USA. It's a great way to sneak in a geography lesson.

174. Go snowshoeing.

175. Bike along a trail. Stop to make dandelion necklaces or to search for bird nests.

176. Tell each other stories. Start by giving the other a starting sentence, such as "I was walking to school the other day when I saw. . . "

177. Create a bead necklace or bracelet.

178. Visit all types of museums: art, science, nature, geology, and so on.

179. Go to local arts and crafts exhibits and shows

180. Volunteer to build a house with Habitat for Humanity, help people at Special Olympics events, or serve Meals on Wheels.

181. Make a fondue meal or a fruit-and-cake fondue for dessert.

182. Take an art class together.

183. Shoot a round of pool.

184. Learn to make homemade root beer or ice cream.

185. Feed the ducks at a park.

Parts of this list were compiled from the books *How to Be Your Little Man's Dad* and *How to Be Your Daughter's Daddy*, written by Dan Bolin and published by Pinon Press, P.O. Box 35007, Colorado Springs, CO 80935 and from Big Brothers Big Sisters of Dane County, Wisconsin. Reprinted with permission.

Endnotes

Chapter 1

1. Henry, Phillip. "An Experience of a Lifetime," 1993. (Submitted to his English class at Baylor.)

2. Henry, Phillip. op. cit.

3. Henry, Phillip. op. cit.

4. Gordon, Kenny. "The American Dream: The Phillip Henry Story," 1994.

5. Beiswinger, George. *One to One: The Story of the Big Brothers/Big Sisters Movement in America,* Philadelphia: Big Brothers Big Sisters of America, 1985.

6. "Big Brothers," *Good Housekeeping.* May 1909.

7. "The First Big Brother," *Modern Maturity.* August–September 1976.

8. Becker, James. *Mentoring High-Risk Kids.* Minneapolis: Johnson Institute, 1994.

Chapter 2

1. "Big Brother mentorship evolves into attachment," *The Commercial Appeal.* Memphis, Tennessee: November 16, 1995.

2. Popenoe, David. *Life Without Father.* New York: The Free Press, 1996.

3. Bassoff, Evelyn S. *Between Mothers and Sons: The Making of Vital and Loving Men.* New York: Plume/Penguin, 1995.

4. Weissbourd, Richard. *The Vulnerable Child.* Reading, Massachusetts: Addison-Wesley, 1996.

5. Gurian, Michael. *The Wonder of Boys.* New York: Tarcher/Putnam, 1996.

6. Bassoff, Evelyn S. op. cit.

Chapter 3

1. "Big Buddies," *Herald Times,* Gaylord, Michigan: October 19, 1995.

2. Peterson, Daneen G. *Big Brothers Big Sisters of America 1994 Agency Demographics Report.* Philadelphia: 1995.

3. Ross, Robert H., and Esther L. Headley. *National Market Research Study on Male Recruitment.* The Research Partnership, The Wichita State University. (Presented at Big Brothers Big Sisters of America's National Conference, 1988.)

4. Corliss, Jean A. "True Brotherhood," *Warren Tribune Chronicle.* Warren, Ohio: October 1, 1995.

Chapter 4

1. "Sharing Big Brother Bonds Fulfills Nathan's Last Wish," *Providence Sunday Journal.* Providence, Rhode Island: 1993.

2. Carter, Ki-Jana, and Scott Gordon. The Big Brothers Big Sisters of America National Conference, Washington, DC: 1996.

3. Big Brothers Big Sisters of Salt Lake City, Utah.

Chapter 5

1. Big Brothers Big Sisters of America National Conference, Washington, DC: 1996.

2. *Tallahassee Democrat,* Tallahassee, Florida: January 30, 1996.

3. Silver, Eric. "I Am Proud to Be Eddie's Big Brother," *Jewish Cleveland News.* Cleveland: 1996.

4. "Big Brothers Impact," *Cape Cod Times.* Hyannis, Massachusetts: August 4, 1995.

Chapter 6

1. "Big Brothers Big Sisters: You Can Make a Difference in a Young Person's Life," *The Herald Bulletin.* Anderson, Indiana: January 20, 1997.

2. Big Brothers Big Sisters of Santa Fe, New Mexico.

3. "Being a Big Brother Fits Volunteer to a Tee." *Chicago Tribune.* November 6, 1996.

4. *The Volunteer.* Big Brothers Big Sisters of South Middlesex, Massachusetts: Summer 1996.

Chapter 7

1. Big Brothers Big Sisters of Sussex County, New Jersey.

2. Gibbs, Debby. "Letter from Mom," Wantage, New Jersey.

3. *Fact Sheet.* Big Brothers Association of Greater Boston: 1995.

4. Roaf, Phoebe, Joseph P. Tierney, and Danista E. I. Hunte. *Big Brothers/Big Sisters: A Study of Volunteer Recruitment and Screening.* Philadelphia: Public/Private Ventures, Fall 1994.

5. *Big Brothers Big Sisters of America 1994 Demographics Report.* 1994.

6. ibid.

7. Howard, Bill. *Matchmaking the Big Brothers/Big Sisters Way.* American Youth Work Center.

Chapter 8

1. *Youth Visions Inc. Annual Report.* Cleveland: 1994.

2. Freedman, Marc. *The Kindness of Strangers: Adult Mentors, Urban Youth and the New Volunteerism.* San Francisco: Jossey Bass, 1993.

3. Big Brothers Big Sisters of Charlotte County, Florida.

Chapter 9

1. "Doing Things the Right Way." *Des Moines Business Record.* Des Moines: July 8, 1996.

2. "A Brother Who Can Spare Kids Some Time," *Chicago Tribune.* April 18, 1993.

Chapter 10

1. Goodman, Ellen. "Mentoring Kids in Crisis." *The Boston Globe.* Boston: March 19, 1995.

2. Freedman, Marc. op. cit.

Appendix I

1. *Uniform Crime Reports, Crime in the United States,* U.S. Department of Justice, Federal Bureau of Investigation, Washington, DC: U.S. Government Printing Office, 1992, 1994.

2. *Juvenile Offenders and Victims: A National Report.* Rockville, Maryland: Juvenile Justice Clearinghouse, 1994.

3. "Drug Use: The National Drug Control Strategy: 1996," Washington DC: Executive Office of the President of the United States, 1996.

4. "National Institute on Drug Abuse, The Monitoring the Future Study" Ann Arbor, Michigan: Institute for Social Research, The University of Michigan.

5. Juvenile Justice Clearinghouse, op. cit.

6. "National Health Interview Survey," Hyattsville, Maryland: U.S. Department of Health and Human Services, National Center for Health Statistics, 1988.

7. Blankenhorn, David. *Fatherless America: Confronting Our Most Urgent Social Problem.* New York: Basic Books, 1995.

8. *1996 Kids Count Data Book.* Baltimore, Maryland: Annie E. Casey Foundation, 1996.

9. Horn, Wade F. PhD. *Father Facts, The National Fatherhood Initiative.* Lancaster, Pennsylvania: 1995.

10. U.S. Department of Health and Human Services, Bureau of the Census.

11. National Prinicipals Association Report on State of High Schools.

12. Cornell, Dewey, et. al. "Characteristics of Adolescents Charged with Homicide," *Behavioral Sciences and the Law* 5. 1987.

13. Davidson, Nicholas. "Life Without Father," *Policy Review* 1990. (See also: Zinsmeister, Karl. "Crime Is Terrorizing Our Nation's Kids," *Citizen* Pamona, California: Focus on the Family, 1990.)

14. Center for Disease Control, Atlanta, Georgia.

15. *Rainbow for All God's Children.*

16. Beck, Allen, Susan Kline, and Lawrence Greenfield. *Survey of Youth in Custody, 1987.* Washington, DC: U.S. Department of Justice, Bureau of Justice Statistics, 1988.

17. Robinson, John P. *How Americans Use Time: A Social-Psychological Analysis of Everyday Behavior.* New York: Praeger, 1977. (See also: John P. Robinson, "Caring for Kids," *American Demographics,* 1989.)

18. Benson, Peter L. *The Troubled Journey: A Portrait of 6th–12th Grade Youth.* Minneapolis, Minnesota: Search Institute, 1993.

19. Horn, Wade F. op. cit.

20. "Who's Minding the Kids?" Washington, DC: U.S. Department of Commerce, Statistical Brief, Bureau of the Census, April 1994.

Appendix II

1. Tierney, Joseph P. and Jean Baldwin Grossman, *Making A Difference: an Impact Study of Big Brothers/Big Sisters.* Philadelphia: Public/Private Ventures, 1995.

2. "Mentoring Keeps Youths On Track; Study Finds Those in Big Brothers-Big Sisters Got In Less Trouble Than Those Who Weren't." *Philadelphia Inquirer,* Philadelphia: 1995.

3. DiTulio, Margaret RN, MBA, and Michael E. Dupre, PhD. *Evaluation Report, Big Brothers Big Sisters of Greater Manchester.* Manchester, New Hampshire: August 1994.

4. *Match, Matchpoint.* Nutmeg Big Brothers Big Sisters Vol. 2., Issue 2, Fall 1996.

Appendix III

1. Bolin, Dan. *How to Be Your Little Man's Dad,* and *How to Be Your Daughter's Daddy.* Colorado Springs, CO: Pinon Press.

Index